Efficient Linux at the Command Line
Boost Your Command-Line Skills

Daniel J. Barrett

Beijing · Boston · Farnham · Sebastopol · Tokyo

Efficient Linux at the Command Line

by Daniel J. Barrett

Published by O'Reilly Media, Inc., 1005 Gravenstein Highway North, Sebastopol, CA 95472.

O'Reilly books may be purchased for educational, business, or sales promotional use. Online editions are also available for most titles (*https://oreilly.com*). For more information, contact our corporate/institutional sales department: 800-998-9938 or *corporate@oreilly.com*.

Acquisitions Editor: John Devins	**Indexer:** Daniel J. Barrett
Development Editor: Virginia Wilson	**Index Editor:** Sue Klefstad
Production Editor: Gregory Hyman	**Interior Designer:** David Futato
Copyeditor: Kim Wimpsett	**Cover Designer:** Karen Montgomery
Proofreader: Piper Editorial Consulting, LLC	**Illustrator:** Kate Dullea

February 2022:   First Edition

Revision History for the First Edition

2022-02-16:	First Release
2022-04-01:	Second Release
2022-10-28:	Third Release
2023-01-06:	Fourth Release
2023-03-31:	Fifth Release
2023-12-08:	Sixth Release
2024-03-01:	Seventh Release

See *https://oreilly.com/catalog/errata.csp?isbn=9781098113407* for release details.

978-1-098-11340-7

[LSI]

Table of Contents

Preface

This book will take your Linux command-line skills to the next level so you can work faster, smarter, and more efficiently.

If you're like most Linux users, you learned your early command-line skills on the job, or by reading an intro book, or by installing Linux at home and just trying things out. I've written this book to help you take the next step—to build intermediate to advanced skills at the Linux command line. It's filled with techniques and concepts that I hope will transform how you interact with Linux and boost your productivity. Think of it as a second book on Linux use that takes you beyond the basics.

A command line is the simplest of interfaces, yet also the most challenging. It's simple because you're presented with nothing but a prompt, which waits for you to run any command you may know:[1]

```
$
```

It's challenging because everything beyond the prompt is your responsibility. There are no friendly icons, buttons, or menus to guide you. Instead, every command you type is a creative act. This is true for basic commands, like listing your files:

```
$ ls
```

and more elaborate commands like this one:

```
$ paste <(echo {1..10}.jpg | sed 's/ /\n/g') \
        <(echo {0..9}.jpg  | sed 's/ /\n/g') \
  | sed 's/^/mv /' \
  | bash
```

If you're staring at the preceding command and thinking, "What the heck is *that*?" or "I would never need such a complex command," then this book is for you.[2]

---

1 This book displays the Linux prompt as a dollar sign. Your prompt may be different.

2 You'll learn this mystery command's purpose in Chapter 8.

What You'll Learn

This book will make you faster and more effective at three essential skills:

- Choosing or constructing commands to solve a business problem at hand
- Running those commands efficiently
- Navigating the Linux filesystem with ease

By the end, you'll understand what happens behind the scenes when you run a command, so you can better predict the results (and not develop superstitions). You'll see a dozen different methods for launching commands and learn when to use each one for best advantage. You'll also learn practical tips and tricks to make you more productive, such as:

- Building complex commands out of simpler ones, step-by-step, to solve real-world problems, such as managing passwords or generating ten thousand test files
- Saving time by organizing your home directory intelligently so you don't have to hunt for files
- Transforming text files and querying them like databases to achieve business goals
- Controlling point-and-click features of Linux from the command line, such as copying and pasting with the clipboard, and retrieving and processing web data, without lifting your hands from the keyboard

Most of all, you'll learn general best practices so no matter which commands you run, you can become more successful in everyday Linux use and more competitive on the job market. This is the book I wish I had when I learned Linux.

What This Book Is Not

This book won't optimize your Linux computer to make it run more efficiently. It makes *you* more efficient at interacting with Linux.

This book is also not a comprehensive reference for the command line—there are hundreds of commands and features that I don't mention. This book is about expertise. It teaches a carefully selected set of command-line knowledge in a practical order to build your skills. For a reference-style guide, try my other book, *Linux Pocket Guide* (O'Reilly).

Audience and Prerequisites

This book assumes you have Linux experience; *it's not an introduction*. It's for users who want to improve their command-line skills, such as students, system administrators, software developers, site reliability engineers, test engineers, and general Linux enthusiasts. Advanced Linux users may find some useful material as well, especially if they learned to run commands by trial and error and want to strengthen their conceptual understanding.

To benefit most from this book, you should already be comfortable with the following topics (if you're not, see Appendix A for a quick refresher):

- Creating and editing text files with a text editor such as vim (vi), emacs, nano, or pico
- Basic file-handling commands such as cp (copy), mv (move or rename), rm (remove or delete), and chmod (change file permissions)
- Basic file-viewing commands such as cat (view an entire file) and less (view one page at a time)
- Basic directory commands such as cd (change directory), ls (list files in a directory), mkdir (create directory), rmdir (remove directory), and pwd (display your current directory name)
- The basics of shell scripts: storing Linux commands in a file, making the file executable (with chmod 755 or chmod +x), and running the file
- Viewing Linux's built-in documentation, known as manpages, with the man command (example: man cat displays documentation on the cat command)
- Becoming the superuser with the sudo command for full access to your Linux system (example: sudo nano /etc/hosts edits the system file */etc/hosts*, which is protected from ordinary users)

If you also know common command-line features such as pattern matching for filenames (with the * and ? symbols), input/output redirection (< and >), and pipes (|), you are off to a good start.

Your Shell

I assume your Linux shell is bash, which is the default shell for most Linux distributions. Whenever I write "the shell," I mean bash. Most of the ideas I present apply to other shells too, such as zsh or dash; see Appendix B to help translate this book's examples for other shells. Much of the material will work unchanged on the Apple Mac Terminal as well, which runs `zsh` by default but can also run `bash`.[3]

Conventions Used in This Book

The following typographical conventions are used in this book:

Italic
> Indicates new terms, URLs, email addresses, filenames, and file extensions.

`Constant width`
> Used for program listings, as well as within paragraphs to refer to program elements such as variable or function names, databases, data types, environment variables, statements, and keywords.

`Constant width bold`
> Shows commands or other text that should be typed literally by the user. Also used occasionally in command output to highlight text of interest.

`Constant width italic`
> Shows text that should be replaced with user-supplied values or by values determined by context. Also used for brief notes on the right side of code listings.

`Constant width highlighted`
> Used in complex program listings to call attention to specific text.

 This element signifies a tip or suggestion.

 This element signifies a general note.

 This element indicates a warning or caution.

---

3 The version of bash on macOS is ancient and missing important features. To upgrade bash, see the article "Upgrading Bash on macOS" (*https://oreil.ly/35jux*) by Daniel Weibel.

Using Code Examples

Supplemental material (code examples, exercises, etc.) is available for download at *https://efficientlinux.com/examples*.

If you have a technical question or a problem using the code examples, please send email to *bookquestions@oreilly.com*.

This book is here to help you get your job done. In general, if example code is offered with this book, you may use it in your programs and documentation. You do not need to contact us for permission unless you're reproducing a significant portion of the code. For example, writing a program that uses several chunks of code from this book does not require permission. Selling or distributing examples from O'Reilly books does require permission. Answering a question by citing this book and quoting example code does not require permission. Incorporating a significant amount of example code from this book into your product's documentation does require permission.

We appreciate, but generally do not require, attribution. An attribution usually includes the title, author, publisher, and ISBN. For example: "*Efficient Linux at the Command Line* by Daniel J. Barrett (O'Reilly). Copyright 2022 Daniel Barrett, 978-1-098-11340-7."

If you feel your use of code examples falls outside fair use or the permission given above, feel free to contact us at *permissions@oreilly.com*.

O'Reilly Online Learning

 For more than 40 years, *O'Reilly Media* has provided technology and business training, knowledge, and insight to help companies succeed.

Our unique network of experts and innovators share their knowledge and expertise through books, articles, and our online learning platform. O'Reilly's online learning platform gives you on-demand access to live training courses, in-depth learning paths, interactive coding environments, and a vast collection of text and video from O'Reilly and 200+ other publishers. For more information, visit *https://oreilly.com*.

How to Contact Us

Please address comments and questions concerning this book to the publisher:

O'Reilly Media, Inc.
1005 Gravenstein Highway North

Sebastopol, CA 95472
800-998-9938 (in the United States or Canada)
707-829-0515 (international or local)
707-829-0104 (fax)

We have a web page for this book, where we list errata, examples, and any additional information. You can access this page at *https://oreil.ly/efficient-linux*.

Email *bookquestions@oreilly.com* to comment or ask technical questions about this book.

For news and information about our books and courses, visit *https://oreilly.com*.

Find us on Facebook: *https://facebook.com/oreilly*

Follow us on Twitter: *https://twitter.com/oreillymedia*

Watch us on YouTube: *https://www.youtube.com/oreillymedia*

Acknowledgments

This book was a joy to write. Thanks to the amazing folks at O'Reilly, especially editors Virginia Wilson and John Devins, production editors Caitlin Ghegan and Gregory Hyman, content manager Kristen Brown, copyeditor Kim Wimpsett, index editor Sue Klefstad, and the ever-helpful tools team. I'm also very grateful to the book's technical reviewers, Paul Bayer, John Bonesio, Dan Ritter, and Carla Schroder, for many insightful comments and criticisms. Thanks also to the Boston Linux Users Group for title suggestions. Special thanks to Maggie Johnson at Google for her kind permission to write the book.

I'd like to offer my deepest thanks to Chip Andrews, Matthew Diaz, and Robert Strandh, who were fellow students at The Johns Hopkins University 35 years ago. They noticed my new and growing interest in Unix and, to my utter surprise, recommended that the Computer Science Department hire me as their next system administrator. Their small act of faith changed the trajectory of my life. (Robert also gets credit for the tip on touch-typing in Chapter 3.) Thanks also to the creators and maintainers of Linux, GNU Emacs, Git, AsciiDoc, and many other open source tools—without these smart and generous people, my career would have been very different indeed.

As always, thank you to my wonderful family, Lisa and Sophia, for their love and patience.

## PART I

Core Concepts

The first four chapters aim to increase your efficiency quickly, covering concepts and techniques that should be immediately useful. You'll learn to combine commands with pipes, understand the responsibilities of the Linux shell, rapidly recall and edit commands from the past, and navigate the Linux filesystem with great speed.

## CHAPTER 1

Combining Commands

When you work in Windows, macOS, and most other operating systems, you probably spend your time running applications like web browsers, word processors, spreadsheets, and games. A typical application is packed with features: everything that the designers thought their users would need. So, most applications are self-sufficient. They don't rely on other apps. You might copy and paste between applications from time to time, but for the most part, they're separate.

The Linux command line is different. Instead of big applications with tons of features, Linux supplies thousands of small commands with very few features. The command cat, for example, prints files on the screen and that's about it. ls lists the files in a directory, mv renames files, and so on. Each command has a simple, fairly well-defined purpose.

What if you need to do something more complicated? Don't worry. Linux makes it easy to *combine commands* so their individual features work together to accomplish your goal. This way of working yields a very different mindset about computing. Instead of asking "Which app should I launch?" to achieve some result, the question becomes "Which commands should I combine?"

In this chapter, you'll learn how to arrange and run commands in different combinations to do what you need. To keep things simple, I'll introduce just six Linux commands and their most basic uses so you can focus on the more complex and interesting part—combining them—without a huge learning curve. It's a bit like learning to cook with six ingredients, or learning carpentry with just a hammer and a saw. (I'll add more commands to your Linux toolbox in Chapter 5.)

You'll combine commands using *pipes*, a Linux feature that connects the output of one command to the input of another. As I introduce each command (wc, head, cut, grep, sort, and uniq), I'll immediately demonstrate its use with pipes. Some examples will be practical for daily Linux use, while others are just toy examples to demonstrate an important feature.

Input, Output, and Pipes

Most Linux commands read input from the keyboard, write output to the screen, or both. Linux has fancy names for this reading and writing:

stdin (pronounced "standard input" or "standard in")
> The stream of input that Linux reads from your keyboard. When you type any command at a prompt, you're supplying data on stdin.

stdout (pronounced "standard output" or "standard out")
> The stream of output that Linux writes to your display. When you run the ls command to print filenames, the results appear on stdout.

Now comes the cool part. You can connect the stdout of one command to the stdin of another, so the first command feeds the second. Let's begin with the familiar ls -l command to list a large directory, such as */bin*, in long format:

```
$ ls -l /bin
total 12104
-rwxr-xr-x 1 root root 1113504 Jun  6  2019 bash
-rwxr-xr-x 1 root root  170456 Sep 21  2019 bsd-csh
-rwxr-xr-x 1 root root   34888 Jul  4  2019 bunzip2
-rwxr-xr-x 1 root root 2062296 Sep 18  2020 busybox
-rwxr-xr-x 1 root root   34888 Jul  4  2019 bzcat
⋮
-rwxr-xr-x 1 root root    5047 Apr 27  2017 znew
```

This directory contains far more files than your display has lines, so the output quickly scrolls off-screen. It's a shame that ls can't print the information one screenful at a time, pausing until you press a key to continue. But wait: another Linux command has that feature. The less command displays a file one screenful at a time:

```
$ less myfile                          View the file; press q to quit
```

You can connect these two commands because ls writes to stdout and less can read from stdin. Use a pipe to send the output of ls to the input of less:

```
$ ls -l /bin | less
```

This combined command displays the directory's contents one screenful at a time. The vertical bar (|) between the commands is the Linux pipe symbol.[1] It connects the

---

1 On US keyboards, the pipe symbol is on the same key as the backslash (\\), usually located between the Enter and Backspace keys or between the left Shift key and Z.

first command's stdout to the next command's stdin. Any command line containing pipes is called a *pipeline*.

Commands generally are not aware that they're part of a pipeline. ls believes it's writing to the display, when in fact its output has been redirected to less. And less believes it's reading from the keyboard when it's actually reading the output of ls.

What's a Command?

The word *command* has three different meanings in Linux, shown in Figure 1-1:

A program
> An executable program named and executed by a single word, such as ls, or a similar feature built into the shell, such as cd (called a *shell builtin*)[2]

A simple command
> A program name (or shell builtin) optionally followed by arguments, such as ls -l /bin

A combined command
> Several simple commands treated as a unit, such as the pipeline ls -l /bin | less

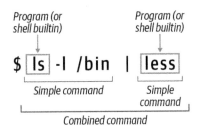

Figure 1-1. Programs, simple commands, and combined commands are all referred to as "commands"

In this book, I'll use the word *command* in all these ways. Usually the surrounding context will make clear which one I mean, but if not, I'll use one of the more specific terms.

---

2 The POSIX standard calls this form of command a *utility*.

Six Commands to Get You Started

Pipes are an essential part of Linux expertise. Let's dive into building your piping skills with a small set of Linux commands so no matter which ones you encounter later, you're ready to combine them.

The six commands—wc, head, cut, grep, sort, and uniq—have numerous options and modes of operation that I'll largely skip for now to focus on pipes. To learn more about any command, run the man command to display full documentation. For example:

```
$ man wc
```

To demonstrate our six commands in action, I'll use a file named *animals.txt* that lists some O'Reilly book information, shown in Example 1-1.

Example 1-1. Inside the file animals.txt

```
python   Programming Python         2010   Lutz, Mark
snail    SSH, The Secure Shell      2005   Barrett, Daniel
alpaca   Intermediate Perl          2012   Schwartz, Randal
robin    MySQL High Availability    2014   Bell, Charles
horse    Linux in a Nutshell        2009   Siever, Ellen
donkey   Cisco IOS in a Nutshell    2005   Boney, James
oryx     Writing Word Macros        1999   Roman, Steven
```

Each line contains four facts about an O'Reilly book, separated by a single tab character: the animal on the front cover, the book title, the year of publication, and the name of the first author.

Command #1: wc

The wc command prints the number of lines, words, and characters in a file:

```
$ wc animals.txt
   7  51 325 animals.txt
```

wc reports that the file *animals.txt* has 7 lines, 51 words, and 325 characters. If you count the characters by eye, including spaces and tabs, you'll find only 318 characters, but wc also includes the invisible newline character that ends each line.

The options -l, -w, and -c instruct wc to print only the number of lines, words, and characters, respectively:

```
$ wc -l animals.txt
7 animals.txt
$ wc -w animals.txt
51 animals.txt
```

```
$ wc -c animals.txt
325 animals.txt
```

Counting is such a useful, general-purpose task that the authors of wc designed the command to work with pipes. It reads from stdin if you omit the filename, and it writes to stdout. Let's use ls to list the contents of the current directory and pipe them to wc to count lines. This pipeline answers the question, "How many files are visible in my current directory?"

```
$ ls -1
animals.txt
myfile
myfile2
test.py
$ ls -1 | wc -l
4
```

The option -1, which tells ls to print its results in a single column, is not strictly necessary here. To learn why I used it, see the sidebar "ls Changes Its Behavior When Redirected" on page 8.

wc is the first command you've seen in this chapter, so you're a bit limited in what you can do with pipes. Just for fun, pipe the output of wc to itself, demonstrating that the same command can appear more than once in a pipeline. This combined command reports that the number of words in the output of wc is four: three integers and a filename:

```
$ wc animals.txt
   7  51 325 animals.txt
$ wc animals.txt | wc -w
4
```

Why stop there? Add a third wc to the pipeline and count lines, words, and characters in the output "4":

```
$ wc animals.txt | wc -w | wc
      1       1       2
```

The output indicates one line (containing the number 4), one word (the number 4 itself), and two characters. Why two? Because the line "4" ends with an invisible newline character.

That's enough silly pipelines with wc. As you gain more commands, the pipelines will become more practical.

ls Changes Its Behavior When Redirected

Unlike virtually every other Linux command, ls is aware of whether stdout is the screen or whether it's been redirected (to a pipe or otherwise). The reason is user-friendliness. When stdout is the screen, ls arranges its output in multiple columns for convenient reading:

```
$ ls /bin
bash        dir        kmod      networkctl      red    tar
bsd-csh     dmesg      less      nisdomainname   rm     tempfile
⋮
```

When stdout is redirected, however, ls produces a single column. I'll demonstrate this by piping the output of ls to a command that simply reproduces its input, such as cat:[3]

```
$ ls /bin | cat
bash
bsd-csh
bunzip2
busybox
⋮
```

This behavior can lead to strange-looking results, as in the following example:

```
$ ls
animals.txt    myfile    myfile2    test.py
$ ls | wc -l
4
```

The first ls command prints all filenames on one line, but the second command reports that ls produced four lines. If you aren't aware of the quirky behavior of ls, you might find this discrepancy confusing.

ls has options to override its default behavior. Force ls to print a single column with the -1 option, or force multiple columns with the -C option.

---

3 Depending on your setup, ls may also use other formatting features, such as color, when printing to the screen but not when redirected.

Command #2: head

The head command prints the first lines of a file. Print the first three lines of *animals.txt* with head using the option -n:

```
$ head -n3 animals.txt
python  Programming Python      2010   Lutz, Mark
snail   SSH, The Secure Shell   2005   Barrett, Daniel
alpaca  Intermediate Perl       2012   Schwartz, Randal
```

If you request more lines than the file contains, head prints the whole file (like cat does). If you omit the -n option, head defaults to 10 lines (-n10).

By itself, head is handy for peeking at the top of a file when you don't care about the rest of the contents. It's a speedy and efficient command, even for very large files, because it needn't read the whole file. In addition, head writes to stdout, making it useful in pipelines. Count the number of words in the first three lines of *animals.txt*:

```
$ head -n3 animals.txt | wc -w
20
```

head can also read from stdin for more pipeline fun. A common use is to reduce the output from another command when you don't care to see all of it, like a long directory listing. For example, list the first five filenames in the */bin* directory:

```
$ ls /bin | head -n5
bash
bsd-csh
bunzip2
busybox
bzcat
```

Command #3: cut

The cut command prints one or more columns from a file. For example, print all book titles from *animals.txt*, which appear in the second column:

```
$ cut -f2 animals.txt
Programming Python
SSH, The Secure Shell
Intermediate Perl
MySQL High Availability
Linux in a Nutshell
Cisco IOS in a Nutshell
Writing Word Macros
```

cut provides two ways to define what a "column" is. The first is to cut by field (-f), when the input consists of strings (fields) each separated by a single tab character. Conveniently, that is exactly the format of the file *animals.txt*. The preceding cut command prints the second field of each line, thanks to the option -f2.

To shorten the output, pipe it to head to print only the first three lines:

```
$ cut -f2 animals.txt | head -n3
Programming Python
SSH, The Secure Shell
Intermediate Perl
```

You can also cut multiple fields, either by separating their field numbers with commas:

```
$ cut -f1,3 animals.txt | head -n3
python   2010
snail    2005
alpaca   2012
```

or by numeric range:

```
$ cut -f2-4 animals.txt | head -n3
Programming Python      2010    Lutz, Mark
SSH, The Secure Shell   2005    Barrett, Daniel
Intermediate Perl       2012    Schwartz, Randal
```

The second way to define a "column" for cut is by character position, using the -c option. Print the first three characters from each line of the file, which you can specify either with commas (1,2,3) or as a range (1-3):

```
$ cut -c1-3 animals.txt
pyt
sna
alp
rob
hor
don
ory
```

Now that you've seen the basic functionality, try something more practical with cut and pipes. Imagine that the *animals.txt* file is thousands of lines long, and you need to extract just the authors' last names. First, isolate the fourth field, author name:

```
$ cut -f4 animals.txt
Lutz, Mark
Barrett, Daniel
Schwartz, Randal
⋮
```

Then pipe the results to cut again, using the option -d (meaning "delimiter") to change the separator character to a comma instead of a tab, to isolate the authors' last names:

```
$ cut -f4 animals.txt | cut -d, -f1
Lutz
Barrett
Schwartz
⋮
```

Save Time with Command History and Editing

Are you retyping a lot of commands? Press the up arrow key instead, repeatedly, to scroll through commands you've run before. (This shell feature is called *command history*.) When you reach the desired command, press Enter to run it immediately, or edit it first using the left and right arrow keys to position the cursor and the Backspace key to delete. (This feature is *command-line editing*.)

I'll discuss much more powerful features for command history and editing in Chapter 3.

Command #4: grep

grep is an extremely powerful command, but for now I'll hide most of its capabilities and say it prints lines that match a given string. (More detail will come in Chapter 5.) For example, the following command displays lines from *animals.txt* that contain the string Nutshell:

```
$ grep Nutshell animals.txt
horse   Linux in a Nutshell      2009    Siever, Ellen
donkey  Cisco IOS in a Nutshell 2005    Boney, James
```

You can also print lines that *don't* match a given string, with the -v option. Notice the lines containing "Nutshell" are absent:

```
$ grep -v Nutshell animals.txt
python  Programming Python       2010    Lutz, Mark
snail   SSH, The Secure Shell    2005    Barrett, Daniel
alpaca  Intermediate Perl        2012    Schwartz, Randal
robin   MySQL High Availability 2014    Bell, Charles
oryx    Writing Word Macros      1999    Roman, Steven
```

In general, grep is useful for finding text in a collection of files. The following command prints lines that contain the string Perl in files with names ending in *.txt*:

```
$ grep Perl *.txt
animals.txt:alpaca      Intermediate Perl       2012    Schwartz, Randal
essay.txt:really love the Perl programming language, which is
essay.txt:languages such as Perl, Python, PHP, and Ruby
```

In this case, grep found three matching lines, one in *animals.txt* and two in *essay.txt*.

grep reads stdin and writes stdout, making it great for pipelines. Suppose you want to know how many subdirectories are in the large directory */usr/lib*. There is no single Linux command to provide that answer, so construct a pipeline. Begin with the ls -l command:

```
$ ls -l /usr/lib
drwxrwxr-x  12 root root    4096 Mar  1 2020 4kstogram
drwxr-xr-x   3 root root    4096 Nov 30 2020 GraphicsMagick-1.4
```

```
drwxr-xr-x    4 root root     4096 Mar 19  2020 NetworkManager
-rw-r--r--    1 root root    35568 Dec  1  2017 attica_kde.so
-rwxr-xr-x    1 root root      684 May  5  2018 cnf-update-db
⋮
```

Notice that ls -l marks directories with a d at the beginning of the line. Use cut to isolate the first column, which may or may not be a d:

```
$ ls -l /usr/lib | cut -c1
d
d
d
-
-
⋮
```

Then use grep to keep only the lines containing d:

```
$ ls -l /usr/lib | cut -c1 | grep d
d
d
d
⋮
```

Finally, count lines with wc, and you have your answer, produced by a four-command pipeline—*/usr/lib* contains 145 subdirectories:

```
$ ls -l /usr/lib | cut -c1 | grep d | wc -l
145
```

Command #5: sort

The sort command reorders the lines of a file into ascending order (the default):

```
$ sort animals.txt
alpaca  Intermediate Perl         2012   Schwartz, Randal
donkey  Cisco IOS in a Nutshell  2005   Boney, James
horse   Linux in a Nutshell       2009   Siever, Ellen
oryx    Writing Word Macros       1999   Roman, Steven
python  Programming Python        2010   Lutz, Mark
robin   MySQL High Availability  2014   Bell, Charles
snail   SSH, The Secure Shell     2005   Barrett, Daniel
```

or descending order (with the -r option):

```
$ sort -r animals.txt
snail   SSH, The Secure Shell     2005   Barrett, Daniel
robin   MySQL High Availability  2014   Bell, Charles
python  Programming Python        2010   Lutz, Mark
oryx    Writing Word Macros       1999   Roman, Steven
horse   Linux in a Nutshell       2009   Siever, Ellen
donkey  Cisco IOS in a Nutshell  2005   Boney, James
alpaca  Intermediate Perl         2012   Schwartz, Randal
```

sort can order the lines alphabetically (the default) or numerically (with the -n option). I'll demonstrate this with pipelines that cut the third field in *animals.txt*, the year of publication:

```
$ cut -f3 animals.txt                    Unsorted
2010
2005
2012
2014
2009
2005
1999
$ cut -f3 animals.txt | sort -n          Ascending
1999
2005
2005
2009
2010
2012
2014
$ cut -f3 animals.txt | sort -nr         Descending
2014
2012
2010
2009
2005
2005
1999
```

To learn the year of the most recent book in *animals.txt*, pipe the output of sort to the input of head and print just the first line:

```
$ cut -f3 animals.txt | sort -nr | head -n1
2014
```

Maximum and Minimum Values

sort and head are powerful partners when working with numeric data, one value per line. You can print the maximum value by piping the data to:

```
... | sort -nr | head -n1
```

and print the minimum value with:

```
... | sort -n | head -n1
```

As another example, let's play with the file */etc/passwd*, which lists the users that can run processes on the system.[4] You'll generate a list of all users in alphabetical order. Peeking at the first five lines, you see something like this:

```
$ head -n5 /etc/passwd
root:x:0:0:root:/root:/bin/bash
daemon:x:1:1:daemon:/usr/sbin:/usr/sbin/nologin
bin:x:2:2:bin:/bin:/usr/sbin/nologin
smith:x:1000:1000:Aisha Smith,,,:/home/smith:/bin/bash
jones:x:1001:1001:Bilbo Jones,,,:/home/jones:/bin/bash
```

Each line consists of strings separated by colons, and the first string is the username, so you can isolate the usernames with the cut command:

```
$ head -n5 /etc/passwd | cut -d: -f1
root
daemon
bin
smith
jones
```

and sort them:

```
$ head -n5 /etc/passwd | cut -d: -f1 | sort
bin
daemon
jones
root
smith
```

To produce the sorted list of all usernames, not just the first five, replace head with cat:

```
$ cat /etc/passwd | cut -d: -f1 | sort
```

To detect if a given user has an account on your system, match their username with grep. Empty output means no account:

```
$ cut -d: -f1 /etc/passwd | grep -w jones
jones
$ cut -d: -f1 /etc/passwd | grep -w rutabaga          (produces no output)
```

The -w option instructs grep to match full words only, not partial words, in case your system also has a username that contains "jones", such as sallyjones2.

Command #6: uniq

The uniq command detects repeated, adjacent lines in a file. By default, it removes the repeats. I'll demonstrate this with a simple file containing capital letters:

---

4 Some Linux systems store the user information elsewhere.

```
$ cat letters
A
A
A
B
B
A
C
C
C
C
$ uniq letters
A
B
A
C
```

Notice that uniq reduced the first three A lines to a single A, but it left the last A in place because it wasn't *adjacent* to the first three.

You can also count occurrences with the -c option:

```
$ uniq -c letters
      3 A
      2 B
      1 A
      4 C
```

I'll admit, when I first encountered the uniq command, I didn't see much use in it, but it quickly became one of my favorites. Suppose you have a tab-separated file of students' final grades for a university course, ranging from A (best) to F (worst):

```
$ cat grades
C        Geraldine
B        Carmine
A        Kayla
A        Sophia
B        Haresh
C        Liam
B        Elijah
B        Emma
A        Olivia
D        Noah
F        Ava
```

You'd like to print the grade with the most occurrences. (If there's a tie, print just one of the winners.) Begin by isolating the grades with cut and sorting them:

```
$ cut -f1 grades | sort
A
A
A
B
```

```
B
B
B
C
C
D
F
```

Next, use `uniq` to count adjacent lines:

```
$ cut -f1 grades | sort | uniq -c
      3 A
      4 B
      2 C
      1 D
      1 F
```

Then sort the lines in reverse order, numerically, to move the most frequently occurring grade to the top line:

```
$ cut -f1 grades | sort | uniq -c | sort -nr
      4 B
      3 A
      2 C
      1 F
      1 D
```

and keep just the first line with `head`:

```
$ cut -f1 grades | sort | uniq -c | sort -nr | head -n1
      4 B
```

Finally, since you want just the letter grade, not the count, isolate the grade with `cut`:

```
$ cut -f1 grades | sort | uniq -c | sort -nr | head -n1 | cut -c9
B
```

and there's your answer, thanks to a six-command pipeline—our longest yet. This sort of step-by-step pipeline construction is not just an educational exercise. It's how Linux experts actually work. Chapter 8 is devoted to this technique.

Detecting Duplicate Files

Let's combine what you've learned with a larger example. Suppose you're in a directory full of JPEG files and you want to know if any are duplicates:

```
$ ls
image001.jpg  image005.jpg  image009.jpg  image013.jpg  image017.jpg
image002.jpg  image006.jpg  image010.jpg  image014.jpg  image018.jpg
⋮
```

You can answer this question with a pipeline. You'll need another command, md5sum, which examines a file's contents and computes a 32-character string called a *checksum*:

```
$ md5sum image001.jpg
146b163929b6533f02e91bdf21cb9563  image001.jpg
```

A given file's checksum, for mathematical reasons, is very, very likely to be unique. If two files have the same checksum, therefore, they are almost certainly duplicates. Here, md5sum indicates the first and third files are duplicates:

```
$ md5sum image001.jpg image002.jpg image003.jpg
146b163929b6533f02e91bdf21cb9563  image001.jpg
63da88b3ddde0843c94269638dfa6958  image002.jpg
146b163929b6533f02e91bdf21cb9563  image003.jpg
```

Duplicate checksums are easy to detect by eye when there are only three files, but what if you have three thousand? It's pipes to the rescue. Compute all the checksums, use cut to isolate the first 32 characters of each line, and sort the lines to make any duplicates adjacent:

```
$ md5sum *.jpg | cut -c1-32 | sort
1258012d57050ef6005739d0e6f6a257
146b163929b6533f02e91bdf21cb9563
146b163929b6533f02e91bdf21cb9563
17f339ed03733f402f74cf386209aeb3
⋮
```

Now add uniq to count repeated lines:

```
$ md5sum *.jpg | cut -c1-32 | sort | uniq -c
      1 1258012d57050ef6005739d0e6f6a257
      2 146b163929b6533f02e91bdf21cb9563
      1 17f339ed03733f402f74cf386209aeb3
⋮
```

If there are no duplicates, all of the counts produced by uniq will be 1. Sort the results numerically from high to low, and any counts greater than 1 will appear at the top of the output:

```
$ md5sum *.jpg | cut -c1-32 | sort | uniq -c | sort -nr
      3 f6464ed766daca87ba407aede21c8fcc
      2 c7978522c58425f6af3f095ef1de1cd5
      2 146b163929b6533f02e91bdf21cb9563
      1 d8ad913044a51408ec1ed8a204ea9502
⋮
```

Now let's remove the nonduplicates. Their checksums are preceded by six spaces, the number one, and a single space. We'll use `grep -v` to remove these lines:[5]

```
$ md5sum *.jpg | cut -c1-32 | sort | uniq -c | sort -nr | grep -v "      1 "
      3 f6464ed766daca87ba407aede21c8fcc
      2 c7978522c58425f6af3f095ef1de1cd5
      2 146b163929b6533f02e91bdf21cb9563
```

Finally, you have your list of duplicate checksums, sorted by the number of occurrences, produced by a beautiful six-command pipeline. If it produces no output, there are no duplicate files.

This command would be even more useful if it displayed the filenames of the duplicates, but that operation requires features we haven't discussed yet. (You'll learn them in "Improving the duplicate file detector" on page 88.) For now, identify the files having a given checksum by searching with `grep`:

```
$ md5sum *.jpg | grep 146b163929b6533f02e91bdf21cb9563
146b163929b6533f02e91bdf21cb9563  image001.jpg
146b163929b6533f02e91bdf21cb9563  image003.jpg
```

and cleaning up the output with `cut`:

```
$ md5sum *.jpg | grep 146b163929b6533f02e91bdf21cb9563 | cut -c35-
image001.jpg
image003.jpg
```

Summary

You've now seen the power of stdin, stdout, and pipes. They turn a small handful of commands into a collection of composable tools, proving that the whole is greater than the sum of the parts. *Any* command that reads stdin or writes stdout can participate in pipelines.[6] As you learn more commands, you can apply the general concepts from this chapter to forge your own powerful combinations.

---

5 Technically, you don't need the final `sort -nr` in this pipeline to isolate duplicates because `grep` removes all the nonduplicates.

6 Some commands do not use stdin/stdout and therefore cannot read from pipes or write to pipes. Examples are `mv` and `rm`. Pipelines may incorporate these commands in other ways, however; you'll see examples in Chapter 8.

## CHAPTER 2

Introducing the Shell

So, you can run commands at a prompt. But what *is* that prompt? Where does it come from, how are your commands run, and why does it matter?

That little prompt is produced by a program called a *shell*. It's a user interface that sits between you and the Linux operating system. Linux supplies several shells, and the most common (and the standard for this book) is called bash. (See Appendix B for notes about other shells.)

bash and other shells do much more than simply run commands. For example, when a command includes a wildcard (*) to refer to multiple files at once:

```
$ ls *.py
data.py    main.py    user_interface.py
```

the wildcard is handled entirely by the shell, not by the program ls. The shell evaluates the expression *.py and invisibly replaces it with a list of matching filenames *before* ls runs. In other words, ls *never sees the wildcard*. From the perspective of ls, you typed the following command:

```
$ ls data.py main.py user_interface.py
```

The shell also handles the pipes you saw in Chapter 1. It redirects stdin and stdout transparently so the programs involved have no idea they are communicating with each other.

Every time a command runs, some steps are the responsibility of the invoked program, such as ls, and some are the responsibility of the shell. Expert users understand which is which. That's one reason they can create long, complex commands off the top of their head and run them successfully. They *already know what the command will do* before they press Enter, in part because they understand the separation between the shell and the programs it invokes.

In this chapter, we'll launch your understanding of the Linux shell. I'll take the same minimalist approach I used for commands and pipes in Chapter 1. Rather than cover dozens of shell features, I'll hand you just enough information to carry you to the next step of your learning journey:

- Pattern matching for filenames
- Variables to store values
- Redirection of input and output
- Quoting and escaping to disable certain shell features
- The search path for locating programs to run
- Saving changes to your shell environment

Shell Vocabulary

The word *shell* has two meanings. Sometimes it means the *concept* of the Linux shell in general, as in "The shell is a powerful tool" or "bash is a shell." Other times it means a specific *instance* of a shell running on a given Linux computer, awaiting your next command.

In this book, the meaning of *shell* should be clear from the context most of the time. When necessary, I'll refer to the second meaning as a *shell instance*, a *running shell*, or your *current shell*.

Some shell instances, but not all, present a prompt so you can interact with them. I'll use the term *interactive shell* to refer to these instances. Other shell instances are non-interactive—they run a sequence of commands and exit.

Pattern Matching for Filenames

In Chapter 1, you worked with several commands that accept filenames as arguments, such as cut, sort, and grep. These commands (and many others) accept multiple filenames as arguments. For example, you can search for the word *Linux* in one hundred files at once, named *chapter1* through *chapter100*:

```
$ grep Linux chapter1 chapter2 chapter3 chapter4 chapter5 ...and so on...
```

Listing multiple files by name is a tedious time-waster, so the shell provides special characters as a shorthand to refer to files or directories with similar names. Many folks call these characters wildcards, but the more general concept is called *pattern matching* or *globbing*. Pattern matching is one of the two most common techniques for speed that Linux users learn. (The other is pressing the up arrow key to recall the shell's previous command, which I describe in Chapter 3.)

Most Linux users are familiar with the star or asterisk character (*), which matches any sequence of zero or more characters (except for a leading dot or a directory slash)[1] in file or directory paths:

```
$ grep Linux chapter*
```

Behind the scenes, the shell (not grep!) expands the pattern chapter* into a list of 100 matching filenames. Then the shell runs grep.

Many users have also seen the question mark (?) special character, which matches any single character (except a leading dot or a directory slash). For example, you could search for the word *Linux* in chapters 1 through 9 only, by providing a single question mark to make the shell match single digits:

```
$ grep Linux chapter?
```

or in chapters 10 through 99, with two question marks to match two digits:

```
$ grep Linux chapter??
```

Fewer users are familiar with square brackets ([]), which request the shell to match a single character from a set. For example, you could search only the first five chapters:

```
$ grep Linux chapter[12345]
```

Equivalently, you could supply a range of characters with a dash:

```
$ grep Linux chapter[1-5]
```

You could also search even-numbered chapters, combining the asterisk and the square brackets to make the shell match filenames ending in an even digit:

```
$ grep Linux chapter*[02468]
```

Any characters, not just digits, may appear within the square brackets for matching. For example, filenames that begin with a capital letter, contain an underscore, and end with an @ symbol would be matched by the shell in this command:

```
$ ls [A-Z]*_*@
```

---

1 That's why the command ls * doesn't list filenames beginning with a dot, a.k.a. dot files.

Terminology: Evaluating Expressions and Expanding Patterns

Strings that you enter on the command line, such as `chapter*` or `Efficient Linux`, are called *expressions*. An entire command like `ls -l chapter*` is an expression too.

When the shell interprets and handles special characters in an expression, such as asterisks and pipe symbols, we say that the shell *evaluates* the expression.

Pattern matching is one kind of evaluation. When the shell evaluates an expression that contains pattern-matching symbols, such as `chapter*`, and replaces it with filenames that match the pattern, we say that the shell *expands* the pattern.

Patterns are valid almost anywhere that you'd supply file or directory paths on the command line. For example, you can list all files in the directory */etc* with names ending in *.conf* using a pattern:

```
$ ls -1 /etc/*.conf
/etc/adduser.conf
/etc/appstream.conf
⋮
/etc/wodim.conf
```

Be careful using a pattern with a command that accepts just one file or directory argument, such as `cd`. You might not get the behavior you expect:

```
$ ls
Pictures    Poems    Politics
$ cd P*                                Three directories will match
bash: cd: too many arguments
```

If a pattern doesn't match any files, the shell leaves it unchanged to be passed literally as a command argument. In the following command, the pattern `*.doc` matches nothing in the current directory, so `ls` looks for a filename literally named `*.doc` and fails:

```
$ ls *.doc
/bin/ls: cannot access '*.doc': No such file or directory
```

When working with file patterns, two points are vitally important to remember. The first, as I've already emphasized, is that the shell, not the invoked program, performs the pattern matching. I know I keep repeating this, but I'm frequently surprised by how many Linux users don't know it and develop superstitions about why certain commands succeed or fail.

The second important point is that shell pattern matching applies only to file and directory paths. It doesn't work for usernames, hostnames, and other types of arguments that certain commands accept. You also cannot type (say) `s?rt` at the beginning of the command line and expect the shell to run the sort program. (Some Linux commands such as grep, sed, and awk perform their own brands of pattern matching, which we'll explore in Chapter 5.)

Filename Pattern Matching and Your Own Programs

All programs that accept filenames as arguments automatically "work" with pattern matching, because the shell evaluates the patterns before the program runs. This is true even for programs and scripts you write yourself. For example, if you wrote a program english2swedish that translated files from English to Swedish and accepted multiple filenames on the command line, you could instantly run it with pattern matching:

```
$ english2swedish *.txt
```

Evaluating Variables

A running shell can define variables and store values in them. A shell variable is a lot like a variable in algebra—it has a name and a value. An example is the shell variable HOME. Its value is the path to your Linux home directory, such as */home/smith*. Another example is USER, whose value is your Linux username, which I'll assume is smith throughout this book.

To print the values of HOME and USER on stdout, run the command printenv:

```
$ printenv HOME
/home/smith
$ printenv USER
smith
```

When the shell evaluates a variable, it replaces the variable name with its value. Simply place a dollar sign in front of the name to evaluate the variable. For example, $HOME evaluates to the string /home/smith.

The easiest way to watch the shell evaluate a command line is to run the echo command, which simply prints its arguments (after the shell is finished evaluating them):

```
$ echo My name is $USER and my files are in $HOME     Evaluating variables
My name is smith and my files are in /home/smith
$ echo ch*ter9                                        Evaluating a pattern
chapter9
```

Where Variables Come From

Variables like USER and HOME are predefined by the shell. Their values are set automatically when you log in. (More on this process later.) Traditionally, such predefined variables have uppercase names.

You also may define or modify a variable anytime by assigning it a value using this syntax:

> name=value

For example, if you work frequently in the directory /home/smith/Projects, you could assign its name to a variable:

```
$ work=$HOME/Projects
```

and use it as a handy shortcut with cd:

```
$ cd $work
$ pwd
/home/smith/Projects
```

You may supply $work to any command that expects a directory:

```
$ cp myfile $work
$ ls $work
myfile
```

When defining a variable, no spaces are permitted around the equals sign. If you forget, the shell will assume (wrongly) that the first word on the command line is a program to run, and the equals sign and value are its arguments, and you'll see an error message:

```
$ work = $HOME/Projects          The shell assumes "work" is a command
work: command not found
```

A user-defined variable like work is just as legitimate and usable as a system-defined variable like HOME. The only practical difference is that some Linux programs change their behavior internally based on the values of HOME, USER, and other system-defined variables. For example, a Linux program with a graphical interface might retrieve your username from the shell and display it. Such programs don't pay attention to an invented variable like work because they weren't programmed to do so.

Variables and Superstition

When you print the value of a variable with echo:

```
$ echo $HOME
/home/smith
```

you might think that the echo command examines the HOME variable and prints its value. That is *not* the case. echo knows nothing about variables. It just prints whatever arguments you hand it. What's really happening is that the shell evaluates $HOME before running echo. From echo's perspective, you typed:

```
$ echo /home/smith
```

This behavior is extremely important to understand, especially as we delve into more complicated commands. The shell evaluates the variables in a command—as well as patterns and other shell constructs—before executing the command.

Patterns Versus Variables

Let's test your understanding of pattern and variable evaluation. Suppose you're in a directory with two subdirectories, *mammals* and *reptiles*, and oddly, the *mammals* subdirectory contains files named *lizard.txt* and *snake.txt*:

```
$ ls
mammals    reptiles
$ ls mammals
lizard.txt  snake.txt
```

In the real world, lizards and snakes are not mammals, so the two files should be moved to the *reptiles* subdirectory. Here are two proposed ways to do it. One works, and one does not:

```
mv mammals/*.txt reptiles                    Method 1

FILES="lizard.txt snake.txt"
mv mammals/$FILES reptiles                    Method 2
```

Method 1 works because patterns match an entire file path. See how the directory name *mammals* is part of both matches for `mammals/*.txt`:

```
$ echo mammals/*.txt
mammals/lizard.txt mammals/snake.txt
```

So, method 1 operates as if you'd typed the following correct command:

```
$ mv mammals/lizard.txt mammals/snake.txt reptiles
```

Method 2 uses variables, which evaluate to their literal value only. They have no special handling for file paths:

```
$ echo mammals/$FILES
mammals/lizard.txt snake.txt
```

So, method 2 operates as if you'd typed the following problematic command:

```
$ mv mammals/lizard.txt snake.txt reptiles
```

This command looks for the file *snake.txt* in the current directory, not in the *mammals* subdirectory, and fails:

```
$ mv mammals/$FILES reptiles
/bin/mv: cannot stat 'snake.txt': No such file or directory
```

To make a variable work in this situation, use a `for` loop that prepends the directory name *mammals* to each filename:

```
FILES="lizard.txt snake.txt"
for f in $FILES; do
  mv mammals/$f reptiles
done
```

Shortening Commands with Aliases

A variable is a name that stands in for a value. The shell also has names that stand in for commands. They're called *aliases*. Define an alias by inventing a name and following it with a equals sign and a command:

```
$ alias g=grep              A command with no arguments
$ alias ll="ls -l"          A command with arguments: quotes are required
```

Run an alias by typing its name as a command. When aliases are shorter than the commands they invoke, you save typing time:

```
$ ll                                        Runs "ls -l"
-rw-r--r-- 1 smith smith 325 Jul  3 17:44 animals.txt
$ g Nutshell animals.txt                    Runs "grep Nutshell animals.txt"
horse   Linux in a Nutshell     2009   Siever, Ellen
donkey  Cisco IOS in a Nutshell 2005   Boney, James
```

 Always define an alias on its own line, not as part of a combined command. (See man bash for the technical details.)

You can define an alias that has the same name as an existing command, effectively replacing that command in your shell. This practice is called *shadowing* the command. Suppose you like the less command for reading files, but you want it to clear the screen before displaying each page. This feature is enabled with the -c option, so define an alias called "less" that runs less -c:[2]

```
$ alias less="less -c"
```

Aliases take precedence over commands of the same name, so you have now shadowed the less command in the current shell. I'll explain what *precedence* means in "Search Path and Aliases" on page 32.

To list a shell's aliases and their values, run alias with no arguments:

```
$ alias
alias g='grep'
alias ll='ls -l'
```

---

2 bash prevents infinite recursion by not expanding the second less as an alias.

To see the value of a single alias, run `alias` followed by its name:

```
$ alias g
alias g='grep'
```

To delete an alias from a shell, run `unalias`:

```
$ unalias g
```

Redirecting Input and Output

The shell controls the input and output of the commands it runs. You've already seen one example: pipes, which direct the stdout of one command to the stdin of another. The pipe syntax, |, is a feature of the shell.

Another shell feature is redirecting stdout to a file. For example, if you use `grep` to print matching lines from the *animals.txt* file from Example 1-1, the command writes to stdout by default:

```
$ grep Perl animals.txt
alpaca   Intermediate Perl     2012     Schwartz, Randal
```

You can send that output to a file instead, using a shell feature called *output redirection*. Simply add the symbol > followed by the name of a file to receive the output:

```
$ grep Perl animals.txt > outfile              (displays no output)
$ cat outfile
alpaca   Intermediate Perl     2012     Schwartz, Randal
```

You have just redirected stdout to the file *outfile* instead of the display. If the file *outfile* doesn't exist, it's created. If it does exist, redirection overwrites its contents. If you'd rather append to the output file rather than overwrite it, use the symbol >> instead:

```
$ grep Perl animals.txt > outfile              Create or overwrite outfile
$ echo There was just one match >> outfile     Append to outfile
$ cat outfile
alpaca   Intermediate Perl     2012     Schwartz, Randal
There was just one match
```

Output redirection has a partner, *input redirection*, that redirects stdin to come from a file instead of the keyboard. Use the symbol < followed by a filename to redirect stdin.

Many Linux commands that accept filenames as arguments, and read from those files, also read from stdin when run with no arguments. An example is `wc` for counting lines, words, and characters in a file:

```
$ wc animals.txt                    Reading from a named file
  7  51 325 animals.txt
$ wc < animals.txt                  Reading from redirected stdin
  7  51 325
```

Standard Error (stderr) and Redirection

In your day-to-day Linux use, you may notice that some output cannot be redirected by >, such as certain error messages. For example, ask cp to copy a file that doesn't exist, and it produces this error message:

```
$ cp nonexistent.txt file.txt
cp: cannot stat 'nonexistent.txt': No such file or directory
```

If you redirect the output (stdout) of this cp command to a file, *errors*, the message still appears on-screen:

```
$ cp nonexistent.txt file.txt > errors
cp: cannot stat 'nonexistent.txt': No such file or directory
```

and the file *errors* is empty:

```
$ cat errors                                    (produces no output)
```

Why does this happen? Linux commands can produce more than one stream of output. In addition to stdout, there is also stderr (pronounced "standard error" or "standard err"), a second stream of output that is traditionally reserved for error messages. The streams stderr and stdout look identical on the display, but internally they are separate. You can redirect stderr with the symbol 2> followed by a filename:

```
$ cp nonexistent.txt file.txt 2> errors
$ cat errors
cp: cannot stat 'nonexistent.txt': No such file or directory
```

and append stderr to a file with 2>> followed by a filename:

```
$ cp nonexistent.txt file.txt 2> errors
$ cp another.txt file.txt 2>> errors
$ cat errors
cp: cannot stat 'nonexistent.txt': No such file or directory
cp: cannot stat 'another.txt': No such file or directory
```

To redirect both stdout and stderr to the same file, use &> followed by a filename:

```
$ echo This file exists > goodfile.txt          Create a file
$ cat goodfile.txt nonexistent.txt &> all.output
$ cat all.output
This file exists
cat: nonexistent.txt: No such file or directory
```

It's *very important* to understand how these two wc commands differ in behavior:

- In the first command, wc receives the filename *animals.txt* as an argument, so wc is aware that the file exists. wc deliberately opens the file on disk and reads its contents.
- In the second command, wc is invoked with no arguments, so it reads from stdin, which is usually the keyboard. The shell, however, sneakily redirects stdin to come from *animals.txt* instead. wc has no idea that the file *animals.txt* exists.

The shell can redirect input and output in the same command:

```
$ wc < animals.txt > count
$ cat count
   7  51 325
```

and can even use pipes at the same time. Here, grep reads from redirected stdin and pipes the results to wc, which writes to redirected stdout, producing the file *count*:

```
$ grep Perl < animals.txt | wc > count
$ cat count
      1       6      47
```

You'll dive deeper into such combined commands in Chapter 8 and see many other examples of redirection throughout the book.

Disabling Evaluation with Quotes and Escapes

Normally the shell uses whitespace as a separator between words. The following command has four words—a program name followed by three arguments:

```
$ ls file1 file2 file3
```

Sometimes, however, you need the shell to treat whitespace as significant, not as a separator. A common example is whitespace in a filename such as *Efficient Linux Tips.txt*:

```
$ ls -l
-rw-r--r-- 1 smith smith 36 Aug  9 22:12 Efficient Linux Tips.txt
```

If you refer to such a filename on the command line, your command may fail because the shell treats the space characters as separators:

```
$ cat Efficient Linux Tips.txt
cat: Efficient: No such file or directory
cat: Linux: No such file or directory
cat: Tips.txt: No such file or directory
```

To force the shell to treat spaces as part of a filename, you have three options—single quotes, double quotes, and backslashes:

```
$ cat 'Efficient Linux Tips.txt'
$ cat "Efficient Linux Tips.txt"
$ cat Efficient\ Linux\ Tips.txt
```

Single quotes tell the shell to treat every character in a string literally, even if the character ordinarily has special meaning to the shell, such as spaces and dollar signs:

```
$ echo '$HOME'
$HOME
```

Double quotes tell the shell to treat all characters literally except for certain dollar signs and a few others you'll learn later:

```
$ echo "Notice that $HOME is evaluated"        Double quotes
Notice that /home/smith is evaluated
$ echo 'Notice that $HOME is not'              Single quotes
Notice that $HOME is not
```

A backslash, also called the *escape character*, tells the shell to treat the next character literally. The following command includes an escaped dollar sign:

```
$ echo \$HOME
$HOME
```

Backslashes act as escape characters even within double quotes:

```
$ echo "The value of \$HOME is $HOME"
The value of $HOME is /home/smith
```

but not within single quotes:

```
$ echo 'The value of \$HOME is $HOME'
The value of \$HOME is $HOME
```

Use the backslash to escape a double quote character within double quotes:

```
$ echo "This message is \"sort of\" interesting"
This message is "sort of" interesting
```

A backslash at the end of a line disables the special nature of the invisible newline character, allowing shell commands to span multiple lines:

```
$ echo "This is a very long message that needs to extend \
onto multiple lines"
This is a very long message that needs to extend onto multiple lines
```

Final backslashes are great for making pipelines more readable, like this one from "Command #6: uniq" on page 14:

```
$ cut -f1 grades \
  | sort \
  | uniq -c \
  | sort -nr \
  | head -n1 \
  | cut -c9
```

When used this way, the backslash is sometimes called a *line continuation character*.

A leading backslash before an alias escapes the alias, causing the shell to look for a command of the same name, ignoring any shadowing:

```
$ alias less="less -c"      Define an alias
$ less myfile               Run the alias, which invokes less -c
$ \less myfile              Run the standard less command, not the alias
```

Locating Programs to Be Run

When the shell first encounters a simple command, such as `ls *.py`, it's just a string of meaningless characters. Quick as a flash, the shell splits the string into two words, "ls" and "*.py". In this case, the first word is the name of a program on disk, and the shell must locate the program to run it.

The program `ls`, it turns out, is an executable file in the directory */bin*. You can verify its location with this command:

```
$ ls -l /bin/ls
-rwxr-xr-x 1 root root 133792 Jan 18  2018 /bin/ls
```

or you can change directories with `cd /bin` and run this lovely, cryptic-looking command:

```
$ ls ls
ls
```

which uses the command `ls` to list the executable file *ls*.

How does the shell locate `ls` in the */bin* directory? Behind the scenes, the shell consults a prearranged list of directories that it holds in memory, called a *search path*. The list is stored as the value of the shell variable PATH:

```
$ echo $PATH
/home/smith/bin:/usr/local/bin:/usr/bin:/bin:/usr/games:/usr/lib/java/bin
```

Directories in a search path are separated by colons (:). For a clearer view, convert the colons to newline characters by piping the output to the tr command, which translates one character into another (more details in Chapter 5):

```
$ echo $PATH | tr : "\n"
/home/smith/bin
/usr/local/bin
/usr/bin
/bin
/usr/games
/usr/lib/java/bin
```

The shell consults directories in your search path from first to last when locating a program like ls. "Does */home/smith/bin/ls* exist? No. Does */usr/local/bin/ls* exist? Nope. How about */usr/bin/ls*? No again! Maybe */bin/ls*? Yes, there it is! I'll run */bin/ls*." This search happens too quickly to notice.[3]

To locate a program in your search path, use the which command:

```
$ which cp
/bin/cp
$ which which
/usr/bin/which
```

or the more powerful (and verbose) type command, a shell builtin that also locates aliases, functions, and shell builtins:[4]

```
$ type cp
cp is hashed (/bin/cp)
$ type ll
ll is aliased to '/bin/ls -l'
$ type type
type is a shell builtin
```

Your search path may contain the same-named command in different directories, such as */usr/bin/less* and */bin/less*. The shell runs whichever command appears in the earlier directory in the path. By leveraging this behavior, you can override a Linux command by placing a same-named command in an earlier directory in your search path, such as your personal *$HOME/bin* directory.

Search Path and Aliases

When the shell searches for a command by name, it checks if that name is an alias before checking the search path. That's why an alias can shadow (take precedence over) a command of the same name.

---

3 Some shells memorize (cache) the paths to programs as they're located, cutting down on future searches.

4 Notice that the command type which produces output, but the command which type does not.

The search path is a great example of taking something mysterious about Linux and showing it has an ordinary explanation. The shell doesn't pull commands out of thin air or locate them by magic. It methodically examines directories in a list until it finds the requested executable file.

Environments and Initialization Files, the Short Version

A running shell holds a bunch of important information in variables: the search path, the current directory, your preferred text editor, your customized shell prompt, and more. The variables of a running shell are collectively called the shell's *environment*. When the shell exits, its environment is destroyed.

It would be extremely tedious to define every shell's environment by hand. The solution is to define the environment once, in shell scripts called *startup files* and *initialization files*, and have every shell execute these scripts on startup. The effect is that certain information appears to be "global" or "known" to all of your running shells.

I'll dive into the gory details in "Configuring Your Environment" on page 103. For now, I'll teach you about one initialization file so you can get through the next few chapters. It's located in your home directory and named *.bashrc* (pronounced "dot bash R C"). Because its name begins with a dot, ls doesn't list it by default:

```
$ ls $HOME
apple    banana    carrot
$ ls -a $HOME
.bashrc    apple    banana    carrot
```

If *$HOME/.bashrc* doesn't exist, create it with a text editor. Commands you place in this file will execute automatically when a shell starts up,[5] so it's a great place to define variables for the shell's environment, and other things important to the shell, such as aliases. Here is a sample *.bashrc* file. Lines beginning with # are comments:

```
# Set the search path
PATH=$HOME/bin:/usr/local/bin:/usr/bin:/bin
# Set the shell prompt
PS1='$ '
# Set your preferred text editor
EDITOR=emacs
# Start in my work directory
cd $HOME/Work/Projects
# Define an alias
alias g=grep
# Offer a hearty greeting
echo "Welcome to Linux, friend!"
```

---

5 This statement is oversimplified; more details are in Table 6-1.

Any changes you make to *$HOME/.bashrc* do not affect any running shells, only future shells. You can force a running shell to reread and execute *$HOME/.bashrc* with either of the following commands:

```
$ source $HOME/.bashrc          Uses the builtin "source" command
$ . $HOME/.bashrc               Uses a dot
```

This process is known as *sourcing* the initialization file. If someone tells you to "source your dot-bash-R-C file," they mean run one of the preceding commands.

 In real life, do not put all of your shell configuration in *$HOME/.bashrc*. Once you've read the details in "Configuring Your Environment" on page 103, examine your *$HOME/.bashrc* and move commands to their proper files as needed.

Summary

I've covered only a tiny number of bash features and their most basic uses. You'll see many more in the chapters that follow, particularly in Chapter 6. For right now, your most important job is to understand the following concepts:

- The shell exists and has important responsibilities.
- The shell evaluates the command line before running any commands.
- Commands can redirect stdin, stdout, and stderr.
- Quoting and escaping prevent special shell characters from being evaluated.
- The shell locates programs using a search path of directories.
- You can change a shell's default behavior by adding commands to the file *$HOME/.bashrc*.

The better you understand the division between the shell and the programs it invokes, the more that the command line will make sense, and the better you can predict what will happen before you press Enter to run a command.

CHAPTER 3

Rerunning Commands

Suppose you've just executed a lengthy command with a detailed pipeline, like this one from "Detecting Duplicate Files" on page 16:

```
$ md5sum *.jpg | cut -c1-32 | sort | uniq -c | sort -nr
```

and you want to run it a second time. Don't retype it! Instead, ask the shell to reach back into history and rerun the command. Behind the scenes, the shell keeps a record of the commands you invoke so you can easily recall and rerun them with a few keystrokes. This shell feature is called *command history*. Expert Linux users make heavy use of command history to speed up their work and avoid wasting time.

Similarly, suppose you make a mistake typing the preceding command before you run it, such as misspelling "jpg" as "jg":

```
$ md5sum *.jg | cut -c1-32 | sort | uniq -c | sort -nr
```

To fix the mistake, don't press the Backspace key dozens of times and retype everything. Instead, change the command in place. The shell supports *command-line editing* for fixing typos and performing all sorts of modifications like a text editor can.

This chapter will show you how to save lots of time and typing by leveraging command history and command-line editing. As usual, I won't attempt to be comprehensive—I'll focus on the most practical and useful parts of these shell features. (If you use a shell other than bash, see Appendix B for additional notes.)

Learn to Touch-Type

All the advice in this book will serve you better if you can type quickly. No matter how knowledgeable you are, if you type 40 words per minute and your equally knowledgeable friend types 120, they're set up to work three times as fast as you. Search the web for "typing speed test" to measure your speed, then search for "typing tutor" and build a lifelong skill. Try to reach 100 words per minute. It's worth the effort.

Viewing the Command History

A *command history* is simply a list of previous commands that you've executed in an interactive shell. To see a shell's history, run the `history` command, which is a shell builtin. The commands appear in chronological order with ID numbers for easy reference. The output looks something like this:

```
$ history
 1000  cd $HOME/Music
 1001  ls
 1002  mv jazz.mp3 jazzy-song.mp3
 1003  play jazzy-song.mp3
   ⋮                              Omitting 477 lines
 1481  cd
 1482  firefox https://google.com
 1483  history                    Includes the command you just ran
```

The output of `history` can be hundreds of lines long (or more). Limit it to the most recent commands by adding an integer argument, which specifies the number of lines to print:

```
$ history 3                       Print the 3 most recent commands
 1482  firefox https://google.com
 1483  history
 1484  history 3
```

Since `history` writes to stdout, you also can process the output with pipes. For example, view your history a screenful at a time:

```
$ history | less                  Earliest to latest entry
$ history | sort -nr | less        Latest to earliest entry
```

or print only the historical commands containing the word cd:

```
$ history | grep -w cd
 1000  cd $HOME/Music
 1092  cd ..
 1123  cd Finances
 1375  cd Checking
```

```
1481  cd
1485  history | grep -w cd
```

To clear (delete) the history for the current shell, use the `-c` option:

```
$ history -c
```

Recalling Commands from the History

I'll show you three time-saving ways to recall commands from a shell's history:

Cursoring
> Extremely simple to learn but often slow in practice

History expansion
> Harder to learn (frankly, it's cryptic) but can be very fast

Incremental search
> Both simple and fast

Each method is best in particular situations, so I recommend learning all three. The more techniques you know, the better you can choose the right one in any situation.

Cursoring Through History

To recall your previous command in a given shell, press the up arrow key. It's that simple. Keep pressing the up arrow to recall earlier commands in reverse chronological order. Press the down arrow to head in the other direction (toward more recent commands). When you reach the desired command, press Enter to run it.

Cursoring through the command history is one of the two most common speedups that Linux users learn. (The other is pattern matching filenames with *, which you saw in Chapter 2.) Cursoring is efficient if your desired command is nearby in the history—no more than two or three commands in the past—but it's tedious to reach commands that are further away. Whacking the up arrow 137 times gets old quickly.

The best use case for cursoring is recalling and running the immediately previous command. On many keyboards, the up arrow key is near the Enter key, so you can press the two keys in sequence with a quick flick of the fingers. On a full-sized American QWERTY keyboard, I place my right ring finger on the up arrow and my right index finger on Enter to tap both keys efficiently. (Try it.)

Frequently Asked Questions About Command History

How many commands are stored in a shell's history?

The maximum is five hundred or whatever number is stored in the shell variable HISTSIZE, which you can change:

```
$ echo $HISTSIZE
500
$ HISTSIZE=10000
```

Computer memory is so cheap and plentiful that it makes sense to set HISTSIZE to a large number so you can recall and rerun commands from the distant past. (A history of 10,000 commands occupies only about 200K of memory.) Or be daring and store unlimited commands by setting the value to -1.

What text is appended to the history?

The shell appends exactly what you type, unevaluated. If you run ls $HOME, the history will contain "ls $HOME", not "ls /home/smith". (There's one exception: see "History Expressions Don't Appear in the Command History" on page 41.)

Are repeated commands appended to the history?

The answer depends on the value of the variable HISTCONTROL. By default, if this variable is unset, then every command is appended. If the value is ignoredups (which I recommend), then repeated commands are not appended if they are consecutive (see man bash for other values):

```
$ HISTCONTROL=ignoredups
```

Does each shell have a separate history, or do all shells share a single history?

Each interactive shell has a separate history.

I launched a new interactive shell and it already has a history. Why?

Whenever an interactive shell exits, it writes its history to the file *$HOME/.bash_history* or whatever path is stored in the shell variable HISTFILE:

```
$ echo $HISTFILE
/home/smith/.bash_history
```

New interactive shells load this file on startup, so they immediately have a history. It's a quirky system if you're running many shells because they *all* write $HISTFILE on exit, so it's a bit unpredictable which history a new shell will load.

The variable HISTFILESIZE controls how many lines of history are written to the file. If you change HISTSIZE to control the size of the history in memory, consider updating HISTFILESIZE as well:

```
$ echo $HISTFILESIZE
500
$ HISTFILESIZE=10000
```

History Expansion

History expansion is a shell feature that accesses the command history using special expressions. The expressions begin with an exclamation point, which traditionally is pronounced "bang." For example, two exclamation points in a row ("bang bang") evaluates to the immediately previous command:

```
$ echo Efficient Linux
Efficient Linux
$ !!                          "Bang bang" = previous command
echo Efficient Linux          The shell helpfully prints the command being run
Efficient Linux
```

To refer to the most recent command that began with a certain string, place an exclamation point in front of that string. So, to rerun the most recent grep command, run "bang grep":

```
$ !grep
grep Perl animals.txt
alpaca   Intermediate Perl      2012    Schwartz, Randal
```

To refer to the most recent command that contained a given string *somewhere*, not just at the beginning of the command, surround the string with question marks as well:[1]

```
$ !?grep?
history | grep -w cd
  1000  cd $HOME/Music
  1092  cd ..
  ⋮
```

You can also retrieve a particular command from a shell's history by its absolute position—the ID number to its left in the output of history. For example, the expression !1203 ("bang 1203") means "the command at position 1203 in the history":

```
$ history | grep hosts
  1203  cat /etc/hosts
$ !1203                           The command at position 1203
cat /etc/hosts
127.0.0.1       localhost
127.0.1.1       example.oreilly.com
::1             example.oreilly.com
```

A negative value retrieves a command by its relative position in the history, rather than absolute position. For example, !-3 ("bang minus three") means "the command you executed three commands ago":

---

1 You can omit the trailing question mark here—!?grep—but in some cases it's required, such as sed-style history expansion (see "More Powerful Substitution with History Expansion" on page 46).

```
$ history
 4197  cd /tmp/junk
 4198  rm *
 4199  head -n2 /etc/hosts
 4199  cd
 4200  history
$ !-3                            The command you executed three commands ago
head -n2 /etc/hosts
127.0.0.1        localhost
127.0.1.1        example.oreilly.com
```

History expansion is quick and convenient, if a bit cryptic. It can be risky, however, if you provide a wrong value and execute it blindly. Look carefully at the preceding example. If you miscounted and typed !-4 instead of !-3, you'd run rm * instead of the intended head command and delete files in your home directory by mistake! To mitigate this risk, append the modifier :p to print the command from your history but not execute it:

```
$ !-3:p
head -n2 /etc/hosts                  Printed, not executed
```

The shell appends the unexecuted command (head) to the history, so if it looks good, you can run it conveniently with a quick "bang bang":

```
$ !-3:p
head -n2 /etc/hosts          Printed, not executed, and appended to history
$ !!                         Run the command for real
head -n2 /etc/hosts          Printed and then executed
127.0.0.1        localhost
127.0.1.1        example.oreilly.com
```

Some people refer to history expansion as "bang commands," but expressions like !! and !grep are not commands. They are string expressions that you can place *anywhere* in a command. As a demonstration, use echo to print the value of !! on stdout without executing it, and count the number of words with wc:

```
$ ls -l /etc | head -n3       Run any command
total 1584
drwxr-xr-x  2 root     root      4096 Jun 16 06:14 ImageMagick-6/
drwxr-xr-x  7 root     root      4096 Mar 19  2020 NetworkManager/

$ echo "!!" | wc -w           Count the words in the previous command
echo "ls -l /etc | head -n3" | wc -w
6
```

This toy example demonstrates that history expansions have more uses than executing commands. You'll see a more practical, powerful technique in the next section.

I've covered only a few features of command history here. For full information, run man history.

History Expressions Don't Appear in the Command History

The shell appends commands to the history verbatim—unevaluated—as I mentioned in "Frequently Asked Questions About Command History" on page 38. The one exception to this rule is history expansion. Its expressions are always evaluated before they're added to the command history:

```
$ ls                    Run any command
hello.txt
$ cd Music              Run some other command
$ !-2                   Use history expansion
ls
song.mp3
$ history               View the history
  1000  ls
  1001  cd Music
  1002  ls              "ls" appears in the history, not "!-2"
  1003  history
```

This exception makes sense. Imagine trying to understand a command history full of expressions like !-15 and !-92 that refer to other history entries. You might have to trace a path through the whole history by eye to understand a single command.

Never Delete the Wrong File Again (Thanks to History Expansion)

Have you ever meant to delete files using a pattern, such as *.txt, but accidentally mistyped the pattern and wiped out the wrong files? Here's an example with an accidental space character after the asterisk:

```
$ ls
123  a.txt  b.txt  c.txt  dont-delete-me  important-file  passwords
$ rm * .txt      DANGER!! Don't run this! Deletes the wrong files!
```

The most common solution to this hazard is to alias rm to run rm -i so it prompts for confirmation before each deletion:

```
$ alias rm='rm -i'              Often found in a shell configuration file
$ rm *.txt
/bin/rm: remove regular file 'a.txt'? y
/bin/rm: remove regular file 'b.txt'? y
/bin/rm: remove regular file 'c.txt'? y
```

As a result, an extra space character needn't be fatal, because the prompts from rm -i will warn that you're removing the wrong files:

```
$ rm * .txt
/bin/rm: remove regular file '123'?      Something is wrong: kill the command
```

The alias solution is cumbersome, however, because most of the time you might not want or need rm to prompt you. It also doesn't work if you're logged into another

Linux machine without your aliases. I'll show you a better way to avoid matching the wrong filenames with a pattern. The technique has two steps and relies on history expansion:

1. *Verify.* Before running rm, run ls with the desired pattern to see which files match.

   ```
   $ ls *.txt
   a.txt    b.txt    c.txt
   ```

2. *Delete.* If the output of ls looks correct, run rm !$ to delete the same files that were matched.[2]

   ```
   $ rm !$
   rm *.txt
   ```

The history expansion !$ ("bang dollar") means "the final word that you typed in the previous command." Therefore, rm !$ here is shorthand for "delete whatever I just listed with ls," namely, *.txt. If you accidentally add a space after the asterisk, the output of ls will make it obvious—safely—that something is wrong:

```
$ ls * .txt
/bin/ls: cannot access '.txt': No such file or directory
123 a.txt    b.txt    c.txt    dont-delete-me    important-file    passwords
```

It's a good thing you ran ls first instead of rm! You can now modify the command to remove the extra space and proceed safely. This two-command sequence—ls followed by rm !$—is a great safety feature to incorporate into your Linux toolbox.

A related technique is peeking at a file's contents with head before you delete it, to make sure you're targeting the right file, and then running rm !$:

```
$ head myfile.txt
(first 10 lines of the file appear)
$ rm !$
rm myfile.txt
```

The shell also provides a history expansion !* ("bang star"), which matches all arguments you typed in the previous command, rather than just the final argument:

```
$ ls *.txt *.o *.log
a.txt    b.txt    c.txt    main.o    output.log    parser.o
$ rm !*
rm *.txt *.o *.log
```

---

2 I'm assuming that no matching files were added or removed behind your back after the ls step. Don't rely on this technique in rapidly changing directories.

In practice, I use !* much less often than !$. Its asterisk carries the same risk of being interpreted as a pattern-matching character for filenames (if you mistype something), so it's not much safer than typing a pattern like *.txt by hand.

Incremental Search of Command History

Wouldn't it be great if you could type a few characters of a command and the rest would appear instantly, ready to run? Well, you can. This speedy feature of the shell, called *incremental search*, is similar to the interactive suggestions provided by web search engines. In most cases, incremental search is the easiest and fastest technique to recall commands from history, even commands you ran long ago. I highly recommend adding it to your toolbox:

1. At the shell prompt, press Ctrl-R (the *R* stands for reverse incremental search).
2. Start typing *any part* of a previous command—beginning, middle, or end.
3. With each character you type, the shell displays the most recent historical command that matches your typing so far.
4. When you see the command you want, press Enter to run it.

Suppose you typed the command cd $HOME/Finances/Bank a while ago and you want to rerun it. Press Ctrl-R at the shell prompt. The prompt changes to indicate an incremental search:

```
(reverse-i-search)`':
```

Start typing the desired command. For example, type c:

```
(reverse-i-search)`': c
```

The shell displays its most recent command that contains the string c, highlighting what you've typed:

```
(reverse-i-search)`': less /etc/hosts
```

Type the next letter, d:

```
(reverse-i-search)`': cd
```

The shell displays its most recent command that contains the string cd, again highlighting what you've typed:

```
(reverse-i-search)`': cd /usr/local
```

Continue typing the command, adding a space and a dollar sign:

```
(reverse-i-search)`': cd $
```

The command line becomes:

```
(reverse-i-search)`': cd $HOME/Finances/Bank
```

This is the command you want. Press Enter to run it, and you're done in five quick keystrokes.

I've assumed here that cd $HOME/Finances/Bank was the most recent matching command in the history. What if it's not? What if you typed a whole bunch of commands that contain the same string? If so, the preceding incremental search would have displayed a different match, such as:

```
(reverse-i-search)`': cd $HOME/Music
```

What now? You could type more characters to hone in on your desired command, but instead, press Ctrl-R a second time. This keystroke causes the shell to jump to the *next* matching command in the history:

```
(reverse-i-search)`': cd $HOME/Linux/Books
```

Keep pressing Ctrl-R until you reach the desired command:

```
(reverse-i-search)`': cd $HOME/Finances/Bank
```

and press Enter to run it.

Here are a few more tricks with incremental search:

- To recall the most recent string that you searched for and executed, begin by pressing Ctrl-R twice in a row.
- To stop an incremental search and continue working on the current command, press the Escape key, or Ctrl-J, or any key for command-line editing (the next topic in this chapter), such as the left or right arrow key.
- To quit an incremental search and clear the command line, press Ctrl-G or Ctrl-C.

Take the time to become expert with incremental search. You'll soon be locating commands with incredible speed.[3]

Command-Line Editing

There are all sorts of reasons to edit a command, either while you type it or after you've run it:

---

3 While writing this book, I frequently reran version-control commands such as git add, git commit, and git push. Incremental search made rerunning these commands a breeze.

- To fix mistakes
- To create a command piece by piece, such as by typing the end of the command first, then moving to the start of the line and typing the beginning
- To construct a new command based on a previous one from your command history (a key skill for building up complex pipelines, as you'll see in Chapter 8)

In this section, I'll show you three ways to edit a command to build your skill and speed:

Cursoring
Again, the slowest and least powerful method but simple to learn

Caret notation
A form of history expansion

Emacs- or Vim-style keystrokes
To edit the command line in powerful ways

As before, I recommend that you learn all three techniques for flexibility.

Cursoring Within a Command

Simply press the left arrow and right arrow keys to move back and forth on the command line, one character at a time. Use the Backspace or Delete key to remove text, and then type any corrections you need. Table 3-1 summarizes these and other standard keystrokes for editing the command line.

Cursoring back and forth is easy but inefficient. It's best when the changes are small and simple.

Table 3-1. Cursor keys for simple command-line editing

Keystroke	Action
Left arrow	Move left by one character
Right arrow	Move right by one character
Ctrl + left arrow	Move left by one word
Ctrl + right arrow	Move right by one word
Home	Move to beginning of command line
End	Move to end of command line
Backspace	Delete one character before the cursor
Delete	Delete one character beneath the cursor

History Expansion with Carets

Suppose you've mistakenly run the following command by typing jg instead of jpg:

```
$ md5sum *.jg | cut -c1-32 | sort | uniq -c | sort -nr
md5sum: '*.jg': No such file or directory
```

To run the command properly, you could recall it from the command history, cursor over to the mistake and fix it, but there's a quicker way to accomplish your goal. Just type the old (wrong) text, the new (corrected) text, and a pair of carets (^), like this:

```
$ ^jg^jpg
```

Press Enter, and the correct command will appear and run:

```
$ ^jg^jpg
md5sum *.jpg | cut -c1-32 | sort | uniq -c | sort -nr
⋮
```

The *caret syntax*, which is a type of history expansion, means, "In the previous command, instead of jg, substitute jpg." Notice that the shell helpfully prints the new command before executing it, which is standard behavior for history expansion.

This technique changes only the first occurrence of the source string (jg) in the command. If your original command contained jg more than once, only the first instance would change to jpg.

More Powerful Substitution with History Expansion

You may be familiar with using the commands sed or ed to change a source string into a target string:

```
s/source/target/
```

The shell also supports a similar syntax. Begin with an expression for history expansion to recall a command, such as !!. Then add a colon, and end with a sed-style substitution. For example, to recall the previous command and replace jg by jpg (first occurrence only), just as caret notation does, run:

```
$ !!:s/jg/jpg/
```

You may begin with any history expansion you like, such as !md5sum, which recalls the most recent command beginning with md5sum, and perform the same replacement of jg by jpg:

```
$ !md5sum:s/jg/jpg/
```

This notation may look complicated, but sometimes it's quicker for achieving your goal than other command-line editing techniques. Run man history for full details.

Emacs- or Vim-Style Command-Line Editing

The most powerful way to edit a command line is with familiar keystrokes inspired by the text editors Emacs and Vim. If you're already skilled with one of these editors, you can jump into this style of command-line editing right away. If not, Table 3-2 will get you started with the most common keystrokes for movement and editing. Note that the Emacs "Meta" key is usually Escape (pressed and released) or Alt (pressed and held).

The shell default is Emacs-style editing, and I recommend it as easier to learn and use. If you prefer Vim-style editing, run the following command (or add it to your *$HOME/.bashrc* file and source it):

```
$ set -o vi
```

To edit a command using Vim keystrokes, press the Escape key to enter command-editing mode, and then use keystrokes from the "Vim" column in Table 3-2. To switch back to Emacs-style editing, run:

```
$ set -o emacs
```

Now practice, practice, practice until the keystrokes (either Emacs's or Vim's) are second nature. Trust me, you'll quickly be paid back in saved time.

Table 3-2. Keystrokes for Emacs- or Vim-style editing[a]

Action	Emacs	Vim
Move forward by one character	Ctrl-f	l
Move backward by one character	Ctrl-b	h
Move forward by one word	Meta-f	w
Move backward by one word	Meta-b	b
Move to beginning of line	Ctrl-a	0
Move to end of line	Ctrl-e	$
Transpose (swap) two characters	Ctrl-t	xp
Transpose (swap) two words	Meta-t	*n/a*
Capitalize word (uppercase first letter)	Meta-c	*n/a*
Uppercase to end of word	Meta-u	*n/a*
Lowercase to end of word	Meta-l	*n/a*
Change case of the current character	*n/a*	~
Insert the next character verbatim, including control characters	Ctrl-v	Ctrl-v
Delete forward by one character	Ctrl-d	x
Delete backward by one character	Backspace *or* Ctrl-h	X
Cut forward by one word	Meta-d	dw
Cut backward by one word	Meta-Backspace *or* Ctrl-w	db

Action	Emacs	Vim
Cut from cursor to beginning of line	Ctrl-u	d^
Cut from cursor to end of line	Ctrl-k	D
Delete the entire line	Ctrl-e Ctrl-u	dd
Paste (yank) the most recently deleted text	Ctrl-y	p
Paste (yank) the next deleted text (after a previous yank)	Meta-y	*n/a*
Undo the previous editing operation	Ctrl-_	u
Undo all edits made so far	Meta-r	U
Switch from insertion mode to command mode	*n/a*	Escape
Switch from command mode to insertion mode	*n/a*	i
Abort an edit operation in progress	Ctrl-g	*n/a*
Clear the display	Ctrl-l	Ctrl-l

[a] Actions marked *n/a* have no simple keystroke but may be possible with longer sequences of keystrokes.

For more details on Emacs-style editing, see the section "Bindable Readline Commands" (*https://oreil.ly/rAQ9g*) in GNU's `bash` manual. For Vim-style editing, see the document "Readline VI Editing Mode Cheat Sheet" (*https://oreil.ly/Zv0ba*).

Summary

Practice the techniques in this chapter and you'll speed up your command-line use immensely. Three of the techniques in particular transformed the way I use Linux, and I hope they will for you too:

- Deleting files with !$ for safety
- Incremental search with Ctrl-R
- Emacs-style command-line editing

CHAPTER 4

Cruising the Filesystem

In the movie *The Adventures of Buckaroo Banzai Across the 8th Dimension*, a classic cult comedy from 1984, the swashbuckling title character offers the following Zen-like words of wisdom: "Remember, no matter where you go…there you are." Buckaroo could very well have been talking about the Linux filesystem:

```
$ cd /usr/share/lib/etc/bin          No matter where you go...
$ pwd
/usr/share/lib/etc/bin               ...there you are.
```

It's also the case that wherever you are in the Linux filesystem—your current directory—you will eventually go somewhere else (to another directory). The faster and more efficiently you can perform this navigation, the more productive you can be.

The techniques in this chapter will help you navigate the filesystem more quickly with less typing. They look deceptively simple but have *enormous* bang for the buck, with small learning curves and big payoffs. These techniques fall into two broad categories:

- Moving quickly to a specific directory
- Returning rapidly to a directory you've visited before

For a quick refresher on Linux directories, see Appendix A. If you use a shell other than `bash`, see Appendix B for additional notes.

Visiting Specific Directories Efficiently

If you ask 10 Linux experts what is the most tedious aspect of the command line, seven of them will say, "Typing long directory paths."[1] After all, if your work files are in */home/smith/Work/Projects/Apps/Neutron-Star/src/include*, your financial documents are in */home/smith/Finances/Bank/Checking/Statements*, and your videos are in */data/Arts/Video/Collection*, it's no fun to retype these paths over and over. In this section, you'll learn techniques to navigate to a given directory efficiently.

Jump to Your Home Directory

Let's begin with the basics. No matter where you go in the filesystem, you can return to your home directory by running cd with no arguments:

```
$ pwd
/etc                               Start somewhere else
$ cd                               Run cd with no arguments...
$ pwd
/home/smith                        ...and you're home again
```

To jump to subdirectories within your home directory from anywhere in the filesystem, refer to your home directory with a shorthand rather than an absolute path such as */home/smith*. One shorthand is the shell variable HOME:

```
$ cd $HOME/Work
```

Another is a tilde:

```
$ cd ~/Work
```

Both $HOME and ~ are expressions expanded by the shell, a fact that you can verify by echoing them to stdout:

```
$ echo $HOME ~
/home/smith /home/smith
```

The tilde can also refer to another user's home directory if you place it immediately in front of their username:

```
$ echo ~jones
/home/jones
```

---

1 I made this up, but it's surely true.

Move Faster with Tab Completion

When you're entering `cd` commands, save typing by pressing the Tab key to produce directory names automatically. As a demonstration, visit a directory that contains subdirectories, such as */usr*:

```
$ cd /usr
$ ls
bin  games  include  lib  local  sbin  share  src
```

Suppose you want to visit the subdirectory *share*. Type `sha` and press the Tab key once:

```
$ cd sha<Tab>
```

The shell completes the directory name for you:

```
$ cd share/
```

This handy shortcut is called *tab completion*. It works immediately when the text that you've typed matches a single directory name. When the text matches multiple directory names, your shell needs more information to complete the desired name. Suppose you had typed only `s` and pressed Tab:

```
$ cd s<Tab>
```

The shell cannot complete the name *share* (yet) because other directory names begin with `s` too: *sbin* and *src*. Press Tab a second time and the shell prints all possible completions to guide you:

```
$ cd s<Tab><Tab>
sbin/  share/  src/
```

and waits for your next action. To resolve the ambiguity, type another character, `h`, and press Tab once:

```
$ cd sh<Tab>
```

The shell completes the name of the directory for you, from *sh* to *share*:

```
$ cd share/
```

In general, press Tab once to perform as much completion as possible, or press twice to print all possible completions. The more characters you type, the less ambiguity and the better the match.

Tab completion is great for speeding up navigation. Instead of typing a lengthy path like */home/smith/Projects/Web/src/include*, type as little as you want and keep pressing the Tab key. You'll get the hang of it quickly with practice.

Tab Completion Varies by Program

Tab completion isn't just for cd commands. It works for most commands, though its behavior may differ. When the command is cd, the Tab key completes directory names. For other commands that operate on files, such as cat, grep, and sort, tab completion expands filenames too. If the command is ssh (secure shell), it completes hostnames. If the command is chown (change the owner of a file), it completes usernames. You can even create your own completion rules for speed, as we'll see in Example 4-1. Also see man bash and read its topic "programmable completion."

Hop to Frequently Visited Directories Using Aliases or Variables

If you visit a faraway directory frequently, such as */home/smith/Work/Projects /Web/src/include*, create an alias that performs the cd operation:

```
# In a shell configuration file:
alias work="cd $HOME/Work/Projects/Web/src/include"
```

Simply run the alias anytime to reach your destination:

```
$ work
$ pwd
/home/smith/Work/Projects/Web/src/include
```

Alternatively, create a variable to hold the directory path:

```
$ work=$HOME/Work/Projects/Web/src/include
$ cd $work
$ pwd
/home/smith/Work/Projects/Web/src/include
$ ls $work/css                           Use the variable in other ways
main.css  mobile.css
```

Edit Frequently Edited Files with an Alias

Sometimes, the reason for visiting a directory frequently is to edit a particular file. If that's the case, consider defining an alias to edit that file by absolute path without changing directory. The following alias definition lets you edit *$HOME/.bashrc*, no matter where you are in the filesystem, by running rcedit. No cd is required:

```
# Place in a shell configuration file and source it:
alias rcedit='$EDITOR $HOME/.bashrc'
```

If you regularly visit lots of directories with long paths, you can create aliases or variables for each of them. This approach has some disadvantages, however:

- It's hard to remember all those aliases/variables.
- You might accidentally create an alias with the same name as an existing command, causing a conflict.

An alternative is to create a shell function like the one in Example 4-1, which I've named qcd ("quick cd"). This function accepts a string key as an argument, such as work or recipes, and runs cd to a selected directory path.

Example 4-1. A function for cd-ing to faraway directories

```
# Define the qcd function
qcd () {
  # Accept 1 argument that's a string key, and perform a different
  # "cd" operation for each key.
  case "$1" in
    work)
      cd $HOME/Work/Projects/Web/src/include
      ;;
    recipes)
      cd $HOME/Family/Cooking/Recipes
      ;;
    video)
      cd /data/Arts/Video/Collection
      ;;
    beatles)
      cd $HOME/Music/mp3/Artists/B/Beatles
      ;;
    *)
      # The supplied argument was not one of the supported keys
      echo "qcd: unknown key '$1'"
      return 1
      ;;
  esac
  # Helpfully print the current directory name to indicate where you are
  pwd
}
# Set up tab completion
complete -W "work recipes video beatles" qcd
```

Store the function in a shell configuration file such as *$HOME/.bashrc* (see "Environments and Initialization Files, the Short Version" on page 33), source it, and it's ready to run. Type qcd followed by one of the supported keys to quickly visit the associated directory:

```
$ qcd beatles
/home/smith/Music/mp3/Artists/B/Beatles
```

As a bonus, the script's final line runs the command `complete`, a shell builtin that sets up customized tab completion for qcd, so it completes the four supported keys. Now you don't have to remember qcd's arguments! Just type qcd followed by a space and press the Tab key twice, and the shell will print all the keys for your reference, and you can complete any of them in the usual way:

```
$ qcd <Tab><Tab>
beatles  recipes  video    work
$ qcd v<Tab><Enter>                    Completes 'v' to 'video'
/data/Arts/Video/Collection
```

Make a Big Filesystem Feel Smaller with CDPATH

The qcd function handles only the directories that you specify. The shell provides a more general cd-ing solution without this shortcoming, called a *cd search path*. This shell feature transformed how I navigate the Linux filesystem.

Suppose you have an important subdirectory that you visit often, named *Photos*. It's located at */home/smith/Family/Memories/Photos*. As you cruise around the filesystem, anytime you want to get to the *Photos* directory, you may have to type a long path, such as:

```
$ cd ~/Family/Memories/Photos
```

Wouldn't it be great if you could shorten this path to just *Photos*, no matter where you are in the filesystem, and reach your subdirectory?

```
$ cd Photos
```

Normally, this command would fail:

```
bash: cd: Photos: No such file or directory
```

unless you happen to be in the correct parent directory (*~/Family/Memories*) or some other directory with a *Photos* subdirectory by coincidence. Well, with a little setup, you can instruct cd to search for your *Photos* subdirectory in locations other than your current directory. The search is lightning fast and looks only in parent directories that you specify. For example, you could instruct cd to search *$HOME/Family/Memories* in addition to the current directory. Then, when you type cd Photos from elsewhere in the filesystem, cd will succeed:

```
$ pwd
/etc
$ cd Photos
/home/smith/Family/Memories/Photos
```

A cd search path works like your command search path, $PATH, but instead of finding commands, it finds subdirectories. Configure it with the shell variable CDPATH, which has the same format as PATH: a list of directories separated by colons. If your CDPATH consists of these four directories, for example:

```
$HOME:$HOME/Projects:$HOME/Family/Memories:/usr/local
```

and you type:

```
$ cd Photos
```

then cd will check the existence of the following directories in order, until it finds one or it fails entirely:

1. *Photos* in the current directory
2. *$HOME/Photos*
3. *$HOME/Projects/Photos*
4. *$HOME/Family/Memories/Photos*
5. */usr/local/Photos*

In this case, cd succeeds on its fourth try and changes directory to *$HOME/Family/Memories/Photos*. If two directories in $CDPATH have a subdirectory named *Photos*, the earlier parent wins.

Ordinarily, a successful cd prints no output. When cd locates a directory using your CDPATH, however, it prints the absolute path on stdout to inform you of your new current directory:

```
$ CDPATH=/usr      Set a CDPATH
$ cd /tmp          No output: CDPATH wasn't consulted
$ cd bin           cd consults CDPATH...
/usr/bin           ...and prints the new working directory
```

Fill CDPATH with your most important or frequently used parent directories, and you can cd into any of their subdirectories from anywhere in the filesystem, no matter how deep they are, without typing most of the path. Trust me, this is *awesome*, and the following case study should prove it.

Organize Your Home Directory for Fast Navigation

Let's use CDPATH to simplify the way you navigate your home directory. With a little configuration, you can make many directories within your home directory easily accessible with minimal typing, no matter where you are in the filesystem. This technique works best if your home directory is well organized with at least two levels of subdirectories. Figure 4-1 shows an example of a well-organized directory layout.

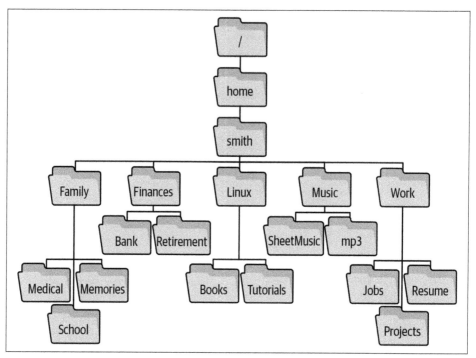

Figure 4-1. Two levels of subdirectories in the directory /home/smith

The trick is to set up your CDPATH to include, in order:

1. $HOME

2. Your choice of subdirectories of $HOME

3. The relative path for a parent directory, indicated by two dots (..)

By including $HOME, you can jump immediately to any of its subdirectories (*Family, Finances, Linux, Music,* and *Work*) from anywhere else in the filesystem without typing a leading path:

```
$ pwd
/etc                              Begin outside your home directory
$ cd Work
/home/smith/Work
$ cd Family/School                You jumped 1 level below $HOME
/home/smith/Family/School
```

By including subdirectories of $HOME in your CDPATH, you can jump into *their* subdirectories in one shot:

```
$ pwd
/etc                              Anywhere outside your home directory
```

```
$ cd School
/home/smith/Family/School          You jumped 2 levels below $HOME
```

All the directories in your CDPATH so far are absolute paths in $HOME and its subdirectories. By including the relative path .. however, you empower new cd behavior in *every* directory. No matter where you are in the filesystem, you can jump to any *sibling* directory (../*sibling*) by name without typing the two dots, because cd will search your current parent. For example, if you're in */usr/bin* and want to move to */usr/lib*, all you need is cd lib:

```
$ pwd
/usr/bin                           Your current directory
$ ls ..
bin    include   lib   src         Your siblings
$ cd lib
/usr/lib                           You jumped to a sibling
```

Or, if you're a programmer working on code that has subdirectories *src*, *include*, and *docs*:

```
$ pwd
/usr/src/myproject
$ ls
docs    include   src
```

you can jump between the subdirectories concisely:

```
$ cd docs                          Change your current directory
$ cd include
/usr/src/myproject/include         You jumped to a sibling
$ cd src
/usr/src/myproject/src             Again
```

A CDPATH for the tree in Figure 4-1 might contain six items: your home directory, four of its subdirectories, and the relative path for a parent directory:

```
# Place in a shell configuration file and source it:
export CDPATH=$HOME:$HOME/Work:$HOME/Family:$HOME/Linux:$HOME/Music:..
```

After sourcing the configuration file, you can cd to a large number of important directories without typing long directory paths, just short directory names. Hooray!

This technique works best if all subdirectories beneath the CDPATH directories have unique names. If you have duplicate names, such as *$HOME/Music* and *$HOME/Linux/Music*, you might not get the behavior you want. The command cd Music will always check *$HOME* before *$HOME/Linux* and consequently will not locate *$HOME/Linux/Music* by search.

To check for duplicate subdirectory names in the first two levels of $HOME, try this brash one-liner. It lists all subdirectories and sub-subdirectories of $HOME, isolates the sub-subdirectory names with cut, sorts the list, and counts occurrences with uniq:

```
$ cd
$ (ls -d */ && ls -d */*/ | cut -d/ -f2-) | sort | uniq -c | sort -nr | less
```

You may recognize this duplicate-checking technique from "Detecting Duplicate Files" on page 16. If the output displays any counts greater than 1, you have duplicates. I realize this command includes a few features I haven't covered yet. You'll learn double ampersand (&&) in "Technique #1: Conditional Lists" on page 108 and the parentheses in "Technique #10: Explicit Subshells" on page 129.

Returning to Directories Efficiently

You've just seen how to visit a directory efficiently. Now I'll show you how to revisit a directory quickly when you need to go back.

Toggle Between Two Directories with "cd -"

Suppose you're working in a deep directory and you run cd to go somewhere else:

```
$ pwd
/home/smith/Finances/Bank/Checking/Statements
$ cd /etc
```

and then think, "No, wait, I want to go back to the *Statements* directory where I just was." Don't retype the long directory path. Just run cd with a dash as an argument:

```
$ cd -
/home/smith/Finances/Bank/Checking/Statements
```

This command returns your shell to its previous directory and helpfully prints its absolute path so you know where you are.

To jump back and forth between a pair of directories, run cd - repeatedly. This is a time-saver when you're doing focused work in two directories in a single shell. There's a catch, however: the shell remembers just one previous directory at a time. For example, if you are toggling between */usr/local/bin* and */etc*:

```
$ pwd
/usr/local/bin
$ cd /etc            The shell remembers /usr/local/bin
$ cd -               The shell remembers /etc
/usr/local/bin
$ cd -               The shell remembers /usr/local/bin
/etc
```

and you run cd without arguments to jump to your home directory:

```
$ cd                 The shell remembers /etc
```

the shell has now forgotten */usr/local/bin* as a previous directory:

```
$ cd -              The shell remembers your home directory
/etc
$ cd -              The shell remembers /etc
/home/smith
```

The next technique overcomes this limitation.

Toggle Among Many Directories with pushd and popd

The `cd` - command toggles between two directories, but what if you have three or more to keep track of? Suppose you're creating a local website on your Linux computer. This task often involves four or more directories:

- The location of live, deployed web pages, such as */var/www/html*
- The web-server configuration directory, often */etc/apache2*
- The location of SSL certificates, often */etc/ssl/certs*
- Your work directory, such as *~/Work/Projects/Web/src*

Believe me, it's tedious to keep typing:

```
$ cd ~/Work/Projects/Web/src
$ cd /var/www/html
$ cd /etc/apache2
$ cd ~/Work/Projects/Web/src
$ cd /etc/ssl/certs
```

If you have a large, windowing display, you can ease the burden by opening a separate shell window for each directory. But if you're working in a single shell (say, over an SSH connection), take advantage of a shell feature called a *directory stack*. It lets you quickly travel among multiple directories with ease, using the built-in shell commands pushd, popd, and dirs. The learning curve is maybe 15 minutes, and the huge payoff in speed lasts a lifetime.[2]

A *directory stack* is a list of directories that you've visited in the current shell and decided to keep track of. You manipulate the stack by performing two operations called *pushing* and *popping*. Pushing a directory adds it to the beginning of the list, which is traditionally called the *top* of the stack. Popping removes the topmost directory from the stack.[3] Initially, the stack contains only your current directory, but you can add (push) and remove (pop) directories and rapidly cd among them.

---

2 An alternative is to open multiple virtual displays using command-line programs like screen and tmux, which are called *terminal multiplexers*. They're more effort to learn than directory stacks but worth a look.

3 If you know stacks from computer science, a directory stack is precisely a stack of directory names.

Every running shell maintains its own directory stack.

I'll begin with the basic operations (pushing, popping, viewing) and then get to the good stuff.

Push a directory onto the stack

The command pushd (short for "push directory") does all of the following:

1. Adds a given directory to the top of the stack
2. Performs a cd to that directory
3. Prints the stack from top to bottom for your reference

I'll build a directory stack of four directories, pushing them onto the stack one at a time:

```
$ pwd
/home/smith/Work/Projects/Web/src
$ pushd /var/www/html
/var/www/html ~/Work/Projects/Web/src
$ pushd /etc/apache2
/etc/apache2 /var/www/html ~/Work/Projects/Web/src
$ pushd /etc/ssl/certs
/etc/ssl/certs /etc/apache2 /var/www/html ~/Work/Projects/Web/src
$ pwd
/etc/ssl/certs
```

The shell prints the stack after each pushd operation. The current directory is the left-most (top) directory.

View a directory stack

Print a shell's directory stack with the dirs command. It does not modify the stack:

```
$ dirs
/etc/ssl/certs /etc/apache2 /var/www/html ~/Work/Projects/Web/src
```

If you prefer to print the stack from top to bottom, use the -p option:

```
$ dirs -p
/etc/ssl/certs
/etc/apache2
/var/www/html
~/Work/Projects/Web/src
```

and even pipe the output to the command nl to number the lines from zero onward:

```
$ dirs -p | nl -v0
     0  /etc/ssl/certs
     1  /etc/apache2
     2  /var/www/html
     3  ~/Work/Projects/Web/src
```

Even simpler, run dirs -v to print the stack with numbered lines:

```
$ dirs -v
 0  /etc/ssl/certs
 1  /etc/apache2
 2  /var/www/html
 3  ~/Work/Projects/Web/src
```

If you prefer this top-down format, consider making an alias:

```
# Place in a shell configuration file and source it:
alias dirs='dirs -v'
```

Pop a directory from the stack

The popd command ("pop directory") is the reverse of pushd. It does all of the following:

1. Removes one directory from the top of the stack

2. Performs a cd to the new top directory

3. Prints the stack from top to bottom for your reference

For example, if your stack has four directories:

```
$ dirs
/etc/ssl/certs /etc/apache2 /var/www/html ~/Work/Projects/Web/src
```

then repeatedly running popd will traverse these directories from top to bottom:

```
$ popd
/etc/apache2 /var/www/html ~/Work/Projects/Web/src
$ popd
/var/www/html ~/Work/Projects/Web/src
$ popd
~/Work/Projects/Web/src
$ popd
bash: popd: directory stack empty
$ pwd
~/Work/Projects/Web/src
```

The pushd and popd commands are such time-savers that I recommend creating two-character aliases that are as quick to type as cd:

```
# Place in a shell configuration file and source it:
alias gd=pushd
alias pd=popd
```

Swap directories on the stack

Now that you can build and empty the directory stack, let's focus on practical use cases. pushd with no arguments swaps the top two directories in the stack and navigates to the new top directory. Let's jump between */etc/apache2* and your work directory several times by simply running pushd. See how the third directory */var/www/html* remains in the stack as the first two directories swap positions:

```
$ dirs
/etc/apache2 ~/Work/Projects/Web/src /var/www/html
$ pushd
~/Work/Projects/Web/src /etc/apache2 /var/www/html
$ pushd
/etc/apache2 ~/Work/Projects/Web/src /var/www/html
$ pushd
~/Work/Projects/Web/src /etc/apache2 /var/www/html
```

Notice that pushd behaves similarly to the cd - command, toggling between two directories, but it does not have the limitation of remembering just one directory.

Turn a mistaken cd into a pushd

Suppose you are jumping among several directories with pushd and you accidentally run cd instead and lose a directory:

```
$ dirs
~/Work/Projects/Web/src /var/www/html /etc/apache2
$ cd /etc/ssl/certs
$ dirs
/etc/ssl/certs /var/www/html /etc/apache2
```

Oops, the accidental cd command replaced *~/Work/Projects/Web/src* in the stack with */etc/ssl/certs*. But don't worry. You can add the missing directory back to the stack without typing its long path. Just run pushd twice, once with a dash argument and once without:

```
$ pushd -
~/Work/Projects/Web/src /etc/ssl/certs /var/www/html /etc/apache2
$ pushd
/etc/ssl/certs ~/Work/Projects/Web/src /var/www/html /etc/apache2
```

Let's dissect why this works:

- The first pushd returns to your shell's previous directory, *~/Work/Projects/Web/src*, and pushes it onto the stack. pushd, like cd, accepts a dash as an argument to mean "go back to my previous directory."

- The second pushd command swaps the top two directories, bringing you back to */etc/ssl/certs*. The end result is that you've restored *~/Work/Projects/Web/src* to the second position in the stack, exactly where it would have been if you hadn't made your mistake.

This "oops, I forgot a pushd" command is useful enough that it's worth an alias. I call it slurp because in my mind, it "slurps back" a directory that I lost by mistake:

```
# Place in a shell configuration file and source it:
alias slurp='pushd - && pushd'
```

Go deeper into the stack

What if you want to cd between directories in the stack other than the top two? pushd and popd accept a positive or negative integer argument to operate further into the stack. The command:

```
$ pushd +N
```

shifts *N* directories from the top of the stack to the bottom and then performs a cd to the new top directory. A negative argument (*-N*) shifts directories in the opposite direction, from the bottom to the top, before performing the cd.[4]

```
$ dirs
/etc/ssl/certs ~/Work/Projects/Web/src /var/www/html /etc/apache2
$ pushd +1
~/Work/Projects/Web/src /var/www/html /etc/apache2 /etc/ssl/certs
$ pushd +2
/etc/apache2 /etc/ssl/certs ~/Work/Projects/Web/src /var/www/html
```

In this manner, you can jump to any other directory in the stack with a simple command. If your stack is long, however, it may be difficult to judge a directory's numeric position by eye. So, print the numeric position of each directory with dirs -v, as you did in "View a directory stack" on page 60:

```
$ dirs -v
0   /etc/apache2
1   /etc/ssl/certs
2   ~/Work/Projects/Web/src
3   /var/www/html
```

---

4 Programmers may recognize these operations as rotating the stack.

To shift */var/www/html* to the top of the stack (and make it your current directory), run pushd +3.

To jump to the directory at the bottom of the stack, run pushd -0 (dash zero):

```
$ dirs
/etc/apache2 /etc/ssl/certs ~/Work/Projects/Web/src /var/www/html
$ pushd -0
/var/www/html /etc/apache2 /etc/ssl/certs ~/Work/Projects/Web/src
```

You also can remove directories from the stack beyond the top directory, using popd with a numeric argument. The command:

```
$ popd +N
```

removes the directory in position *N* from the stack, counting down from the top. A negative argument (-*N*) counts up from the bottom of the stack instead. Counting begins at zero, so popd +1 removes the second directory from the top:

```
$ dirs
/var/www/html /etc/apache2 /etc/ssl/certs ~/Work/Projects/Web/src
$ popd +1
/var/www/html /etc/ssl/certs ~/Work/Projects/Web/src
$ popd +2
/var/www/html /etc/ssl/certs
```

Summary

All of the techniques in this chapter are easy to grasp with a bit of practice and will save you lots of time and typing. The techniques I've found particularly life changing are:

- CDPATH for rapid navigation
- pushd and popd for rapid returns
- The occasional cd - command

PART II
Next-Level Skills

Now that you understand the basics of commands, pipes, the shell, and navigation, it's time to take the next step. In the following five chapters, I'll present an abundance of new Linux programs and some important shell concepts. You'll apply them to construct complex commands and tackle realistic situations on a Linux computer.

## CHAPTER 5

Expanding Your Toolbox

Linux systems come with thousands of command-line programs. Experienced users typically rely on a smaller subset—a toolbox of sorts—that they return to again and again. Chapter 1 added six highly useful commands to your toolbox, and now I'll hand you about a dozen more. I'll describe each command briefly and show you some example uses. (To see all available options, view a command's manpage.) I'll also introduce two powerful commands that are harder to learn but well worth the effort, called awk and sed. Overall, the commands in this chapter serve four common, practical needs for pipelines and other complex commands:

Producing text
> Printing dates, times, sequences of numbers and letters, file paths, repeated strings, and other text to jumpstart your pipelines.

Isolating text
> Extracting any part of a text file with a combination of grep, cut, head, tail, and one handy feature of awk.

Combining text
> Combining files from top to bottom with cat and tac, or side by side with echo and paste. You can also interleave files with paste and diff.

Transforming text
> Converting text into other text using simple commands such as tr and rev, or more powerful commands such as awk and sed.

This chapter is a quick overview. Later chapters show the commands in action.

Producing Text

Every pipeline begins with a simple command that prints to stdout. Sometimes it's a command like `grep` or `cut` that pulls selected data from a file:

```
$ cut -d: -f1 /etc/passwd | sort      Print all usernames and sort them
```

or even `cat`, which is convenient for piping the full contents of multiple files to other commands:

```
$ cat *.txt | wc -l                   Total the number of lines
```

Other times, the initial text in a pipeline comes from other sources. You already know one such command, `ls`, which prints file and directory names and associated information. Let's take a look at some other text-producing commands and techniques:

date
>   Prints dates and times in various formats

seq
>   Prints a sequence of numbers

Brace expansion
>   A shell feature that prints a sequence of numbers or characters

find
>   Prints file paths

yes
>   Prints the same line repeatedly

The date Command

The `date` command prints the current date and/or time in various formats:

```
$ date                         Default formatting
Mon Jun 28 16:57:33 EDT 2021
$ date +%Y-%m-%d               Year-Month-Day format
2021-06-28
$ date +%H:%M:%S               Hour:Minute:Seconds format
16:57:33
```

To control the output format, provide an argument that begins with a plus sign (+) followed by any text. The text may contain special expressions that begin with a percent sign (%), such as `%Y` for the current four-digit year and `%H` for the current hour on a 24-hour clock. A full list of expressions is on the manpage for `date`.

```
$ date +"I cannot believe it's already %A!"      Day of week
I cannot believe it's already Tuesday!
```

The seq Command

The `seq` command prints a sequence of numbers in a range. Provide two arguments, the low and high values of the range, and `seq` prints the whole range:

```
$ seq 1 5              Print all integers from 1 to 5, inclusive
1
2
3
4
5
```

If you provide three arguments, the first and third define the range, and the middle number is the increment:

```
$ seq 1 2 10           Increment by 2 instead of 1
1
3
5
7
9
```

Use a negative increment such as `-1` to produce a descending sequence:

```
$ seq 3 -1 0
3
2
1
0
```

or a decimal increment to produce floating-point numbers:

```
$ seq 1.1 0.1 2        Increment by 0.1
1.1
1.2
1.3
⋮
2.0
```

By default, values are separated by a newline character, but you can change the separator with the `-s` option followed by any string:

```
$ seq -s/ 1 5          Separate values with forward slashes
1/2/3/4/5
```

The option `-w` makes all values the same width (in characters) by adding leading zeros as needed:

```
$ seq -w 8 10
08
09
10
```

seq can produce numbers in many other formats (see the manpage), but my examples represent the most common uses.

Brace Expansion (A Shell Feature)

The shell provides its own way to print a sequence of numbers, known as *brace expansion*. Start with a left curly brace, add two integers separated by two dots, and end with a right curly brace:

```
$ echo {1..10}                          Forward from 1
1 2 3 4 5 6 7 8 9 10
$ echo {10..1}                          Backward from 10
10 9 8 7 6 5 4 3 2 1
$ echo {01..10}                         With leading zeros (equal width)
01 02 03 04 05 06 07 08 09 10
```

More generally, the shell expression {x..y..z} generates the values x through y, incrementing by z:

```
$ echo {1..1000..100}                   Count by hundreds from 1
1 101 201 301 401 501 601 701 801 901
$ echo {1000..1..100}                   Backward from 1000
1000 900 800 700 600 500 400 300 200 100
$ echo {01..1000..100}                  With leading zeros
0001 0101 0201 0301 0401 0501 0601 0701 0801 0901
```

Curly Braces Versus Square Brackets

Square brackets are a pattern-matching operator for filenames (Chapter 2). Curly brace expansion, on the other hand, does not depend on filenames in any way. It just evaluates to a list of strings. You can use brace expansion to *print* filenames, but no pattern matching occurs:

```
$ ls
file1 file2 file4
$ ls file[2-4]                  Matches existing filenames
file2 file4
$ ls file{2..4}                 Evaluates to: file2 file3 file4
ls: cannot access 'file3': No such file or directory
file2  file4
```

Brace expansion also can produce sequences of letters, which seq cannot:

```
$ echo {A..Z}
A B C D E F G H I J K L M N O P Q R S T U V W X Y Z
```

Brace expansion always produces output on a single line separated by space characters. Change this by piping the output to other commands, such as `tr` (see "The tr Command" on page 83):

```
$ echo {A..Z} | tr -d ' '          Delete spaces
ABCDEFGHIJKLMNOPQRSTUVWXYZ
$ echo {A..Z} | tr ' ' '\n'        Change spaces into newlines
A
B
C
⋮
Z
```

Create an alias that prints the nth letter of the English alphabet:

```
$ alias nth="echo {A..Z} | tr -d ' ' | cut -c"
$ nth 10
J
```

The find Command

The `find` command lists files in a directory recursively, descending into subdirectories and printing full paths.[1] Results are not alphabetical (pipe the output to `sort` if needed):

```
$ find /etc -print          List all of /etc recursively
/etc
/etc/issue.net
/etc/nanorc
/etc/apache2
/etc/apache2/sites-available
/etc/apache2/sites-available/default.conf
⋮
```

`find` has numerous options that you can combine. Here are a few highly useful ones. Limit the output only to files or directories with the option `-type`:

```
$ find . -type f -print          Files only
$ find . -type d -print          Directories only
```

Limit the output to names that match a filename pattern with the option `-name`. Quote or escape the pattern so the shell doesn't evaluate it first:

```
$ find /etc -type f -name "*.conf" -print          Files ending with .conf
/etc/logrotate.conf
/etc/systemd/logind.conf
/etc/systemd/timesyncd.conf
⋮
```

---

1 The related command `ls -R` produces output in a format that's less convenient for pipelines.

Make the name-matching case insensitive with the option -iname:

```
$ find . -iname "*.txt" -print
```

find has sensible defaults. The default directory is the current directory, and the default action is -print, so the following commands are equivalent:

```
$ find . -iname "*.txt" -print
$ find -iname "*.txt"
```

find can also execute a Linux command for *each file path* in the output, using -exec. The syntax is a bit wonky:

1. Construct a find command and omit -print.

2. Append -exec followed by the command to execute. Use the expression {} to indicate where the file path should appear in the command.

3. End with a quoted or escaped semicolon, such as ";" or \;.

Here's a toy example to print an @ symbol on either side of the file path:

```
$ find /etc -exec echo @ {} @ ";"
@ /etc @
@ /etc/issue.net @
@ /etc/nanorc @
⋮
```

A more practical example performs a long listing (ls -l) for all *.conf* files in */etc* and its subdirectories:

```
$ find /etc -type f -name "*.conf" -exec ls -l {} ";"
-rw-r--r-- 1 root root 703  Aug 21  2017 /etc/logrotate.conf
-rw-r--r-- 1 root root 1022 Apr 20  2018 /etc/systemd/logind.conf
-rw-r--r-- 1 root root 604  Apr 20  2018 /etc/systemd/timesyncd.conf
⋮
```

find -exec works well for mass deletions of files throughout a directory hierarchy (but be careful!). Let's delete files with names ending in a tilde (~) within the directory *$HOME/tmp* and its subdirectories. For safety, first run the command echo rm to see which files would be deleted, then remove echo to delete for real:

```
$ find $HOME/tmp -type f -name "*~" -exec echo rm {} ";"        echo for safety
rm /home/smith/tmp/file1~
rm /home/smith/tmp/junk/file2~
rm /home/smith/tmp/vm/vm-8.2.0b/lisp/vm-cus-load.el~
$ find $HOME/tmp -type f -name "*~" -exec rm {} ";"             Delete for real
```

find also has some built-in actions, such as -ls to list files and -delete to remove them, that are more efficient than -exec ls or -exec rm:

```
$ find /etc -type f -name "*.conf" -ls          List .conf files like "ls -l"
$ find $HOME/tmp -type f -name "*~" -delete     Delete tilde files
```

The yes Command

The yes command prints the same string over and over until terminated:

```
$ yes            Repeats "y" by default
y
y
y ^C             Kill the command with Ctrl-C
$ yes woof!      Repeat any other string
woof!
woof!
woof! ^C
```

What's the use of this curious behavior? yes can supply input to interactive programs so they can run unattended. For example, the program fsck, which checks a Linux filesystem for errors, may prompt the user to continue and wait for a response of y or n. The output of the yes command, when piped to fsck, responds to every prompt on your behalf, so you can walk away and let fsck run to completion.[2]

The main use of yes for our purposes is printing a string a specific number of times by piping yes to head (you'll see a practical example in "Generating Test Files" on page 147):

```
$ yes "Efficient Linux" | head -n3        Print a string 3 times
Efficient Linux
Efficient Linux
Efficient Linux
```

Isolating Text

When you need just part of a file, the simplest commands to combine and run are grep, cut, head, and tail. You've already seen the first three in Chapter 1: grep prints lines that match a string, cut prints columns from a file, and head prints the first lines of a file. A new command, tail, is the opposite of head and prints the last lines of a file. Figure 5-1 depicts these four commands working together.

---

2 Nowadays, some implementations of fsck have options -y and -n to respond yes or no, respectively, to every prompt, so the yes command is unnecessary here.

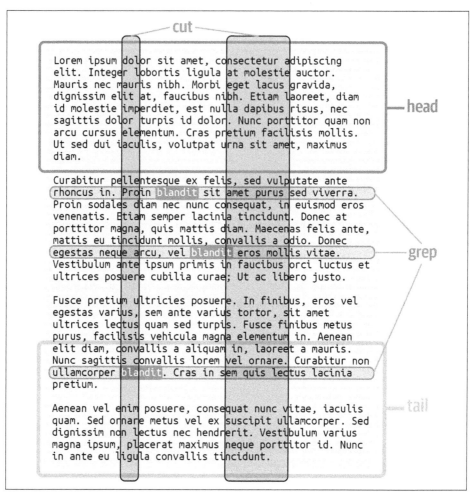

Figure 5-1. head, grep, and tail extract lines, and cut extracts columns. In this exam-ple, grep matches lines containing the string "blandit."

In this section, I dive more deeply into grep, which does a lot more than match plain strings, and explain tail more formally. I also preview one feature of the command awk for extracting columns in a way that cut cannot. These five commands in combi-nation can isolate pretty much any text using a single pipeline.

grep: A Deeper Look

You've already seen grep print lines from a file that match a given string:

```
$ cat frost
Whose woods these are I think I know.
His house is in the village though;
```

```
He will not see me stopping here
To watch his woods fill up with snow.
This is not the end of the poem.
$ grep his frost                          Print lines containing "his"
To watch his woods fill up with snow.
This is not the end of the poem.          "This" matches "his"
```

grep also has some highly useful options. Use the -w option to match whole words only:

```
$ grep -w his frost                       Match the word "his" exactly
To watch his woods fill up with snow.
```

Use the -i option to ignore the case of letters:

```
$ grep -i his frost
His house is in the village though;       Matches "His"
To watch his woods fill up with snow.     Matches "his"
This is not the end of the poem.          "This" matches "his"
```

Use the -l option to print only the names of the files that contain matching lines, but not the matching lines themselves:

```
$ grep -l his *          Which files contain the string "his"?
frost
```

The real power of grep, however, appears when you move beyond matching simple strings to matching patterns, called *regular expressions*.[3] The syntax is different from filename patterns; a partial description is in Table 5-1.

Table 5-1. Some regular expression syntax shared by grep, awk, and sed[a]

To match this:	Use this syntax:	Example
Beginning of a line	^	^a = Line beginning with a
End of a line	$	!$ = Line ending with an exclamation point
Any single character (except newline)	.	... = Any three consecutive characters
A literal caret, dollar sign, or any other special character c	\c	\$ = A literal dollar sign
Zero or more occurrences of expression E	E*	_* = Zero or more underscores
Any single character in a set	[characters]	[aeiouAEIOU] = Any vowel
Any single character *not* in a set	[^characters]	[^aeiouAEIOU] = Any nonvowel
Any character in a given range between c_1 and c_2	[c_1-c_2]	[0-9] = Any digit
Any character *not* in a given range between c_1 and c_2	[^c_1-c_2]	[^0-9] = Any nondigit

---

3 The name *grep* is short for "get regular expression and print."

To match this:	Use this syntax:	Example
Either of two expressions E_1 or E_2	$E_1 \backslash \| E_2$ for grep and sed	one\\\|two = Either one or two
	$E_1 \| E_2$ for awk	one | two = Either one or two
Grouping expression E for precedence	$\backslash(E\backslash)$ for grep and sed [b]	\\(one\\\|two\\)* = Zero or more occurrences of one or two
	(E) for awk	(one|two)* = Zero or more occurrences of one or two

[a] The three commands also differ in their treatment of regular expressions; Table 5-1 presents a partial list.

[b] For sed, this syntax does more than grouping; see "Matching subexpressions with sed" on page 92.

Here are some example grep commands with regular expressions. Match all lines that begin with a capital letter:

```
$ grep '^[A-Z]' myfile
```

Match all nonblank lines (i.e., match blank lines and use -v to omit them):

```
$ grep -v '^$' myfile
```

Match all lines that contain either *cookie* or *cake*:

```
$ grep 'cookie\|cake' myfile
```

Match all lines at least five characters long:

```
$ grep '.....' myfile
```

Match all lines in which a less-than symbol appears somewhere before a greater-than symbol, such as lines of HTML code:

```
$ grep '<.*>' page.html
```

Regular expressions are great, but sometimes they get in the way. Suppose you want to search for the two lines in the *frost* file that contain a w followed by a period. The following command produces the wrong results, because a period is a regular expression meaning "any character":

```
$ grep w. frost
Whose woods these are I think I know.
He will not see me stopping here
To watch his woods fill up with snow.
```

To work around this problem, you can escape the special character:

```
$ grep 'w\.' frost
Whose woods these are I think I know.
To watch his woods fill up with snow.
```

but this solution becomes cumbersome if you have many special characters to escape. Fortunately, you can force grep to forget about regular expressions and search for every character literally in the input by using the -F ("fixed") option. (You may also run the equivalent fgrep command, but it is officially deprecated.)

```
$ grep -F w. frost
Whose woods these are I think I know.
To watch his woods fill up with snow.
$ fgrep w. frost
Whose woods these are I think I know.
To watch his woods fill up with snow.
```

grep has many other options; I'll present just one more that solves a common problem. Use the -f option (lowercase; don't confuse it with -F) to match against a set of strings rather than a single string. As a practical example, let's list all shells found in the file */etc/passwd*, which I introduced in "Command #5: sort" on page 12. As you may recall, each line in */etc/passwd* contains information about a user, organized as colon-separated fields. The final field on each line is the program launched when the user logs in. This program is often but not always a shell:

```
$ cat /etc/passwd
root:x:0:0:root:/root:/bin/bash          7th field is a shell
daemon:x:1:1:daemon:/usr/sbin:/usr/sbin/nologin     7th field is not a shell
⋮
```

How can you tell if a program is a shell? Well, the file */etc/shells* lists all valid login shells on a Linux system:

```
$ cat /etc/shells
/bin/sh
/bin/bash
/bin/csh
```

So, you can list all valid shells in */etc/passwd* by extracting the seventh field with cut, eliminating duplicates with sort -u, and checking the results against */etc/shells* with grep -f. I also add the -F option to be cautious, so all lines in */etc/shells* are taken literally, even if they contain special characters:

```
$ cut -d: -f7 /etc/passwd | sort -u | grep -f /etc/shells -F
/bin/bash
/bin/sh
```

The tail Command

The tail command prints the last lines of a file—10 lines by default. It's a partner to the head command. Suppose you have a file named *alphabet* containing 26 lines, one per letter:

```
$ cat alphabet
A is for aardvark
B is for bunny
C is for chipmunk
⋮
```

```
X is for xenorhabdus
Y is for yak
Z is for zebu
```

Print the last three lines with `tail`. The option `-n` sets the number of lines to be printed, just as it does for head:

```
$ tail -n3 alphabet
X is for xenorhabdus
Y is for yak
Z is for zebu
```

If you precede the number with a plus sign (+), printing begins at that line number and proceeds to the end of the file. The following command begins at the 25th line of the file:

```
$ tail -n+25 alphabet
Y is for yak
Z is for zebu
```

Combine `tail` and `head` to print any range of lines from a file. To print the fourth line alone, for example, extract the first four lines and isolate the last one:

```
$ head -n4 alphabet | tail -n1
D is for dingo
```

In general, to print lines *M* through *N*, extract the first *N* lines with head, then isolate the last *N-M+1* lines with `tail`. Print lines six through eight of the *alphabet* file:

```
$ head -n8 alphabet | tail -n3
F is for falcon
G is for gorilla
H is for hawk
```

 head and `tail` both support a simpler syntax to specify a number of lines without `-n`. This syntax is ancient, undocumented, and deprecated but will probably remain supported forever:

```
$ head -4 alphabet        Same as head -n4 alphabet
$ tail -3 alphabet        Same as tail -n3 alphabet
$ tail +25 alphabet       Same as tail -n+25 alphabet
```

The awk {print} Command

The command `awk` is a general-purpose text processor with hundreds of uses. Let's preview one small feature, `print`, that extracts columns from a file in ways that `cut` cannot. Consider the system file */etc/hosts*, which includes IP addresses and hostnames separated by any amount of whitespace:

```
$ less /etc/hosts
127.0.0.1       localhost
127.0.1.1           myhost      myhost.example.com
192.168.1.2        frodo
192.168.1.3     gollum
192.168.1.28       gandalf
```

Suppose you want to isolate hostnames by printing the second word on each line. The challenge is that each hostname is preceded by an arbitrary amount of whitespace. cut needs its columns either lined up neatly by column number (-c) or separated by a single consistent character (-f). You need a command to print the second word on each line, which awk provides with ease:

```
$ awk '{print $2}' /etc/hosts
localhost
myhost
frodo
gollum
gandalf
```

awk refers to any column by a dollar sign followed by the column number: for example, $7 for the seventh column. If the column number has more than one digit, surround the number with parentheses: for example, $(25). To refer to the final field, use $NF ("number of fields"). To refer to the entire line, use $0.

awk does not print whitespace between values by default. If you want whitespace, separate the values with commas:

```
$ echo Efficient fun Linux | awk '{print $1 $3}'        No whitespace
EfficientLinux
$ echo Efficient fun Linux | awk '{print $1, $3}'       Whitespace
Efficient Linux
```

awk's print statement is great for processing the output of commands that strays outside tidy columns. An example is df, which prints the amount of free and used disk space on a Linux system:

```
$ df / /data
Filesystem      1K-blocks       Used  Available Use% Mounted on
/dev/sda1      1888543276  902295944  890244772  51% /
/dev/sda2      7441141620 1599844268 5466214400  23% /data
```

The column locations may vary depending on the length of the Filesystem paths, the disk sizes, and the options you pass to df, so you can't reliably extract values with cut. With awk, however, you can easily isolate (say) the fourth value on each line, representing available disk space:

```
$ df / /data | awk '{print $4}'
Available
890244772
5466214400
```

and even remove the first line (the header) at the same time with a little awk magic, printing only line numbers greater than 1:

```
$ df / /data | awk 'FNR>1 {print $4}'
890244772
5466214400
```

If you encounter input separated by something other than space characters, awk can change its field separator to any regular expression with the -F option:

```
$ echo efficient::::::linux | awk -F':*' '{print $2}'        Any number of colons
linux
```

You'll learn more details about awk in "awk essentials" on page 86.

Combining Text

You already know several commands that combine text from different files. The first is cat, which prints the contents of multiple files to stdout. It's a joiner of files top-to-bottom. That's where its name comes from—it con*cat*enates files:

```
$ cat poem1
It is an ancient Mariner,
And he stoppeth one of three.
$ cat poem2
'By thy long grey beard and glittering eye,
$ cat poem3
Now wherefore stopp'st thou me?
$ cat poem1 poem2 poem3
It is an ancient Mariner,
And he stoppeth one of three.
'By thy long grey beard and glittering eye,
Now wherefore stopp'st thou me?
```

The second command you've seen for combining text is echo, the shell builtin that prints whatever arguments you give it, separated by a single space character. It combines strings side by side:

```
$ echo efficient          linux      in      $HOME
efficient linux in /home/smith
```

Let's examine some more commands that combine text:

tac
    A bottom-to-top combiner of text files

paste
    A side-by-side combiner of text files

diff
    A command that interleaves text from two files by printing their differences

The tac Command

The `tac` command reverses a file line by line. Its name is *cat* spelled backward.

```
$ cat poem1 poem2 poem3 | tac
Now wherefore stopp'st thou me?
'By thy long grey beard and glittering eye,
And he stoppeth one of three.
It is an ancient Mariner,
```

Notice I concatenated three files before reversing the text. If I instead provide multiple files to `tac` as arguments, it reverses the lines of each file in turn, producing different output:

```
$ tac poem1 poem2 poem3
And he stoppeth one of three.            First file reversed
It is an ancient Mariner,
'By thy long grey beard and glittering eye,   Second file
Now wherefore stopp'st thou me?          Third file
```

`tac` is great for processing data that is already in chronological order but not reversible with the `sort -r` command. A typical case is reversing a web-server log file to process its lines from newest to oldest:

```
192.168.1.34 - - [30/Nov/2021:23:37:39 -0500] "GET / HTTP/1.1" ...
192.168.1.10 - - [01/Dec/2021:00:02:11 -0500] "GET /notes.html HTTP/1.1" ...
192.168.1.8 - - [01/Dec/2021:00:04:30 -0500] "GET /stuff.html HTTP/1.1" ...
⋮
```

The lines are in chronological order with timestamps, but they aren't in alphabetical or numeric order, so the `sort -r` command isn't helpful. The `tac` command can reverse these lines without needing to consider the timestamps.

The paste Command

The `paste` command combines files side by side in columns separated by a single tab character. It's a partner to the `cut` command, which extracts columns from a tab-separated file:

```
$ cat title-words1
EFFICIENT
AT
COMMAND
$ cat title-words2
linux
the
line
$ paste title-words1 title-words2
EFFICIENT       linux
AT      the
COMMAND line
```

```
$ paste title-words1 title-words2 | cut -f2          cut & paste are complementary
linux
the
line
```

Change the separator to another character, such as a comma, with the option -d (meaning "delimiter"):

```
$ paste -d, title-words1 title-words2
EFFICIENT,linux
AT,the
COMMAND,line
```

Transpose the output, producing pasted rows instead of pasted columns, with the -s option:

```
$ paste -d, -s title-words1 title-words2
EFFICIENT,AT,COMMAND
linux,the,line
```

paste also interleaves data from two or more files if you change the separator to a newline character (\n):

```
$ paste -d "\n" title-words1 title-words2
EFFICIENT
linux
AT
the
COMMAND
line
```

The diff Command

diff compares two files line by line and prints a terse report about their differences:

```
$ cat file1
Linux is all about efficiency.
I hope you will enjoy this book.
$ cat file2
MacOS is all about efficiency.
I hope you will enjoy this book.
Have a nice day.
$ diff file1 file2
1c1
< Linux is all about efficiency.
---
> MacOS is all about efficiency.
2a3
> Have a nice day.
```

The notation 1c1 represents a change or difference between the files. It means that line 1 in the first file differs from line 1 in the second file. This notation is followed by the relevant line from *file1*, a three-dash separator (- - -), and the relevant line from

---

file2. The leading symbol < always indicates a line from the first file, and > indicates a line from the second file.

The notation 2a3 represents an addition. It means that *file2* has a third line not present after the second line of *file1*. This notation is followed by the extra line from *file2*, "Have a nice day."

diff output may contain other notation and can take other forms. This short explanation is enough for our main purpose, however, which is to use diff as a text processor that interleaves lines from two files. Many users don't think of diff this way, but it's great for forming pipelines to solve certain kinds of problems. For example, you can isolate the differing lines with grep and cut:

```
$ diff file1 file2 | grep '^[<>]'
< Linux is all about efficiency.
> MacOS is all about efficiency.
> Have a nice day.
$ diff file1 file2 | grep '^[<>]' | cut -c3-
Linux is all about efficiency.
MacOS is all about efficiency.
Have a nice day.
```

You'll see practical examples in "Technique #4: Process Substitution" on page 112 and "Checking Matched Pairs of Files" on page 143.

Transforming Text

Chapter 1 introduced several commands that read text from stdin and transform it into something else on stdout. wc prints a count of lines, words, and characters; sort arranges lines into alphabetical or numeric order; and uniq consolidates duplicate lines. Let's discuss several more commands that transform their input:

tr
> Translates characters into other characters

rev
> Reverses characters on a line

awk *and* sed
> General-purpose transformers

The tr Command

tr translates one set of characters into another. I showed you one example in Chapter 2 of translating colons into newline characters to print the shell's PATH:

```
$ echo $PATH | tr : "\n"          Translate colons into newlines
/home/smith/bin
```

```
/usr/local/bin
/usr/bin
/bin
/usr/games
/usr/lib/java/bin
```

tr takes two sets of characters as arguments, and it translates members of the first set into the corresponding members of the second. Common uses are converting text to uppercase or lowercase:

```
$ echo efficient | tr a-z A-Z        Translate a into A, b into B, etc.
EFFICIENT
$ echo Efficient | tr A-Z a-z
efficient
```

converting spaces into newlines:

```
$ echo Efficient Linux | tr " " "\n"
Efficient
Linux
```

and deleting whitespace with the -d (delete) option:

```
$ echo efficient linux | tr -d ' \t'      Remove spaces and tabs
efficientlinux
```

The rev Command

The rev command reverses the characters of each line of input:[4]

```
$ echo Efficient Linux! | rev
!xuniL tneiciffE
```

Beyond the obvious entertainment value, rev is handy for extracting tricky information from files. Suppose you have a file of celebrity names:

```
$ cat celebrities
Jamie Lee Curtis
Zooey Deschanel
Zendaya Maree Stoermer Coleman
Rihanna
```

and you want to extract the final word on each line (Curtis, Deschanel, Coleman, Rihanna). This would be easy with cut -f if each line had the same number of fields, but the number varies. With rev, you can reverse all the lines, cut the *first* field, and reverse again to achieve your goal:[5]

---

4 Quiz: what does the pipeline rev myfile | tac | rev | tac do?

5 You'll see simpler solutions with awk and sed shortly, but this double-rev trick is handy to know.

```
$ rev celebrities
sitruC eeL eimaJ
lenahcseD yeooZ
nameloC remreotS eeraM ayadneZ
annahiR
$ rev celebrities | cut -d' ' -f1
sitruC
lenahcseD
nameloC
annahiR
$ rev celebrities | cut -d' ' -f1 | rev
Curtis
Deschanel
Coleman
Rihanna
```

The awk and sed Commands

awk and sed are general-purpose "supercommands" for processing text. They can do
most everything that the other commands in this chapter do, but with more cryptic-
looking syntax. As a simple example, they can print the first 10 lines of a file like head
does:

```
$ sed 10q myfile          Print 10 lines and quit (q)
$ awk 'FNR<=10' myfile    Print while line number is ≤ 10
```

They can also do things that our other commands cannot, like replace or swap
strings:

```
$ echo image.jpg | sed 's/\.jpg/.png/'          Replace .jpg by .png
image.png
$ echo "linux efficient" | awk '{print $2, $1}'   Swap two words
efficient linux
```

awk and sed are harder to learn than the other commands I've covered, because each
of them has a miniature programming language built in. They have so many capabilities that whole books have been written on them.[6] I highly recommend spending
quality time learning both commands (or at least one of them). To begin your journey, I cover basic principles of each command and demonstrate some common uses.
I also recommend several online tutorials to learn more about these powerful, crucial
commands.

Don't worry about memorizing every feature of awk or sed. Success with these commands really means:

---

6 Including the book *sed & awk* from O'Reilly.

- Understanding the *kinds* of transformations they make possible, so you can think, "Ah! This is a job for awk (or sed)!" and apply them in your time of need

- Learning to read their manpages and to find complete solutions on Stack Exchange (*https://oreil.ly/0948M*) and other online resources

awk essentials

awk transforms lines of text from files (or stdin) into any other text, using a sequence of instructions called an *awk program*.[7] The more skilled you become in writing awk programs, the more flexibly you can manipulate text. You can supply the awk program on the command line:

```
$ awk program input-files
```

You can also store one or more awk programs in files and refer to them with the -f option, and the programs run in sequence:

```
$ awk -f program-file1 -f program-file2 -f program-file3 input-files
```

An awk program includes one or more *actions*, such as calculating values or printing text, that run when an input line matches a *pattern*. Each instruction in the program has the form:

```
pattern {action}
```

Typical patterns include:

The word BEGIN
  Its action runs just once, before awk processes any input.

The word END
  Its action runs just once, after awk has processed all the input.

A regular expression (see Table 5-1) surrounded by forward slashes
  An example is /^[A-Z]/ to match lines that begin with a capital letter.

Other expressions specific to awk
  For example, to check whether the third field on an input line ($3) begins with a capital letter, a pattern would be $3~/^[A-Z]/. Another example is FNR>5, which tells awk to skip the first five lines of input.

An action with no pattern runs for every line of input. (Several awk programs in "The awk {print} Command" on page 78 were of this type.) As an example, awk elegantly

---

7 The name *awk* is an acronym for Aho, Weinberger, and Kernighan, the program's creators.

solves the "print the celebrity's last name" problem from "The rev Command" on page 84 by directly printing the final word from each line:

```
$ awk '{print $NF}' celebrities
Curtis
Deschanel
Coleman
Rihanna
```

 When supplying an awk program on the command line, enclose it in quotes to prevent the shell from evaluating awk's special characters. Use single or double quotes as needed.

A pattern with no action runs the default action {print}, which just prints any matching input lines unchanged:

```
$ echo efficient linux | awk '/efficient/'
efficient linux
```

For a fuller demonstration, process the tab-separated file *animals.txt* from Example 1-1 to produce a tidy bibliography, converting lines from this format:

```
python  Programming Python     2010    Lutz, Mark
```

to this format:

```
Lutz, Mark (2010). "Programming Python"
```

This feat requires rearranging three fields and adding some characters like parentheses and double quotes. The following awk program does the trick, employing the option -F to change the input separator from spaces to tabs (\t):

```
$ awk -F'\t' '{print $4, "(" $3 ").", "\"" $2 "\""}' animals.txt
Lutz, Mark (2010). "Programming Python"
Barrett, Daniel (2005). "SSH, The Secure Shell"
Schwartz, Randal (2012). "Intermediate Perl"
Bell, Charles (2014). "MySQL High Availability"
Siever, Ellen (2009). "Linux in a Nutshell"
Boney, James (2005). "Cisco IOS in a Nutshell"
Roman, Steven (1999). "Writing Word Macros"
```

Add a regular expression to process only the "horse" book:

```
$ awk -F'\t' '/^horse/{print $4, "(" $3 ").", "\"" $2 "\""}' animals.txt
Siever, Ellen (2009). "Linux in a Nutshell"
```

Or process only books from 2010 or later, by testing whether field $3 matches ^201:

```
$ awk -F'\t' '$3~/^201/{print $4, "(" $3 ").", "\"" $2 "\""}' animals.txt
Lutz, Mark (2010). "Programming Python"
```

```
        Schwartz, Randal (2012). "Intermediate Perl"
        Bell, Charles (2014). "MySQL High Availability"
```

Finally, add a `BEGIN` instruction to print a friendly heading, some dashes for indenting, and an `END` instruction to direct the reader to further information:

```
$ awk -F'\t' \
  'BEGIN {print "Recent books:"} \
  $3~/^201/{print "-", $4, "(" $3 ").", "\"" $2 "\""} \
  END {print "For more books, search the web"}' \
  animals.txt
Recent books:
- Lutz, Mark (2010). "Programming Python"
- Schwartz, Randal (2012). "Intermediate Perl"
- Bell, Charles (2014). "MySQL High Availability"
For more books, search the web
```

awk does much more than print—it can also perform calculations, like summing the numbers 1 to 100:

```
$ seq 1 100 | awk '{s+=$1} END {print s}'
5050
```

To learn awk beyond what can be covered in a few book pages, take an awk tutorial at tutorialspoint.com/awk or riptutorial.com/awk or search the web for "awk tutorial." You'll be glad you did.

Improving the duplicate file detector

In "Detecting Duplicate Files" on page 16, you constructed a pipeline that detects and counts duplicate JPEG files by checksum, but it was not powerful enough to print the filenames:

```
$ md5sum *.jpg | cut -c1-32 | sort | uniq -c | sort -nr | grep -v "      1 "
      3 f6464ed766daca87ba407aede21c8fcc
      2 c7978522c58425f6af3f095ef1de1cd5
      2 146b163929b6533f02e91bdf21cb9563
```

Now that you know awk, you have the tools to print the filenames as well. Let's construct a new command that reads each line of md5sum output:

```
$ md5sum *.jpg
146b163929b6533f02e91bdf21cb9563  image001.jpg
63da88b3ddde0843c94269638dfa6958  image002.jpg
146b163929b6533f02e91bdf21cb9563  image003.jpg
⋮
```

and not only counts occurrences of each checksum but also stores the filenames for printing. You'll need two additional awk features called *arrays* and *loops*.

An *array* is a variable that holds a collection of values. If the array is named A and holds seven values, then the values could be accessed as A[1], A[2], A[3], up to A[7]. The values 1 through 7 are called the *keys* of the array, and A[1] through A[7] are called the array's *elements*. You can create any keys you want, however. If you'd rather access the seven elements of your array using the names of Disney characters, go ahead and name them A["Doc"], A["Grumpy"], A["Bashful"], all the way to A["Dopey"].

To count duplicate images, create an array called counts with one element for each checksum. Each array key is a checksum, and the associated element holds the number of times that checksum occurs in the input. For example, the array element counts["f6464ed766daca87ba407aede21c8fcc"] could have value 3. The following awk script examines each line of md5sum output, isolates the checksum ($1), and uses it as a key for the counts array. The operator ++ increments an element by 1 each time awk encounters its associated checksum:

```
$ md5sum *.jpg | awk '{counts[$1]++}'
```

So far, the awk script produces no output—it just counts each checksum and exits. To print the counts, you need a second awk feature called a for loop. A for loop steps through an array, key by key, and processes each element in sequence, using this syntax:

```
for (variable in array) do something with array[variable]
```

For example, print each array element by its key:

```
for (key in counts) print array[key]
```

Place this loop in the END instruction so it runs after all the counts are calculated.

```
$ md5sum *.jpg \
  | awk '{counts[$1]++} \
         END { for (key in counts) print counts[key] }'
1
2
2
⋮
```

Next, add the checksums to the output. Each array key is a checksum, so just print the key after the count:

```
$ md5sum *.jpg \
  | awk '{counts[$1]++} \
         END {for (key in counts) print counts[key] " " key }'
1 714eceeb06b43c03fe20eb96474f69b8
2 146b163929b6533f02e91bdf21cb9563
2 c7978522c58425f6af3f095ef1de1cd5
⋮
```

To collect and print filenames, use a second array, names, also with checksums as its keys. As awk processes each line of output, append the filename ($2) to the corresponding element of the names array, along with a space as a separator. In the END loop, after printing the checksum (key), print a colon and the collected filenames for that checksum:

```
$ md5sum *.jpg \
  | awk '{counts[$1]++; names[$1]=names[$1] " " $2} \
         END {for (key in counts) print counts[key] " " key ":" names[key]}'
1 714eceeb06b43c03fe20eb96474f69b8: image011.jpg
2 146b163929b6533f02e91bdf21cb9563: image001.jpg image003.jpg
2 c7978522c58425f6af3f095ef1de1cd5: image019.jpg image020.jpg
⋮
```

Lines that begin with 1 represent checksums that occur only once, so they are not duplicates. Pipe the output to grep -v to remove these lines, then sort the results numerically, high to low, with sort -nr and you have your desired output:

```
$ md5sum *.jpg \
  | awk '{counts[$1]++; names[$1]=names[$1] " " $2} \
         END {for (key in counts) print counts[key] " " key ":" names[key]}' \
  | grep -v '^1 ' \
  | sort -nr
3 f6464ed766daca87ba407aede21c8fcc: image007.jpg image012.jpg image014.jpg
2 c7978522c58425f6af3f095ef1de1cd5: image019.jpg image020.jpg
2 146b163929b6533f02e91bdf21cb9563: image001.jpg image003.jpg
```

sed essentials

sed, like awk, transforms text from files (or stdin) into any other text, using a sequence of instructions called a *sed script*.[8] sed scripts are pretty cryptic on first glance. An example is s/Windows/Linux/g, which means to replace every occurrence of the string Windows with Linux. The word *script* here does not mean a file (like a shell script) but a string.[9] Invoke sed with a single script on the command line:

```
$ sed script input-files
```

or use the -e option to supply multiple scripts that process the input in sequence:

```
$ sed -e script1 -e script2 -e script3 input-files
```

You can also store sed scripts in files and refer to them with the -f option, and they run in sequence:

```
$ sed -f script-file1 -f script-file2 -f script-file3 input-files
```

---

8 The name *sed* is short for "stream editor," because it edits a stream of text.

9 If you're familiar with the editors vi, vim, ex, or ed, sed script syntax may look familiar.

As with `awk`, the utility of `sed` depends on your skill in creating sed scripts. The most common type of script is a substitution script that replaces strings with other strings. The syntax is:

```
s/regexp/replacement/
```

where *regexp* is a regular expression to match against each input line (see Table 5-1), and *replacement* is a string to replace the matched text. As a simple example, change one word into another:

```
$ echo Efficient Windows | sed "s/Windows/Linux/"
Efficient Linux
```

When supplying a sed script on the command line, enclose it in quotes to prevent the shell from evaluating sed's special characters. Use single or double quotes as needed.

sed easily solves the "print the celebrity's last name" problem from "The rev Command" on page 84 with a regular expression. Just match all characters (`.*`) up to the last space and replace them with nothing:

```
$ sed 's/.* //' celebrities
Curtis
Deschanel
Coleman
Rihanna
```

Substitution and Slashes

The forward slashes in a substitution may be replaced by any other convenient character. This is helpful when a regular expression itself includes forward slashes (which would otherwise need escaping). These three sed scripts are equivalent:

```
s/one/two/      s_one_two_      s@one@two@
```

You may follow a substitution with several options to affect its behavior. The option `i` makes matches case insensitive:

```
$ echo Efficient Stuff | sed "s/stuff/linux/"      Case sensitive; no match
Efficient Stuff
$ echo Efficient Stuff | sed "s/stuff/linux/i"     Case-insensitive match
Efficient linux
```

The option `g` ("global") replaces all occurrences of the regular expression instead of just the first one:

```
$ echo efficient stuff | sed "s/f/F/"        Replaces just the first "f"
eFficient stuff
$ echo efficient stuff | sed "s/f/F/g"       Replaces all occurrences of "f"
eFFicient stuFF
```

Another common type of sed script is a deletion script. It removes lines by their line number:

```
$ seq 10 14 | sed 4d                   Remove the 4th line
10
11
12
14
```

or lines that match a regular expression:

```
$ seq 101 200 | sed '/[13579]$/d'     Delete lines ending in an odd digit
102
104
106
⋮
200
```

Matching subexpressions with sed

Suppose you have some filenames:

```
$ ls
image.jpg.1  image.jpg.2  image.jpg.3
```

and want to produce new names, *image1.jpg*, *image2.jpg*, and *image3.jpg*. sed can split the filenames into parts and rearrange them via a feature called *subexpressions*. First, create a regular expression that matches the filenames:

```
image\.jpg\.[1-3]
```

You want to move the final digit earlier in the filename, so isolate that digit by surrounding it with the symbols \(and \). This defines a subexpression—a designated part of a regular expression:

```
image\.jpg\.\([1-3]\)
```

sed can refer to subexpressions by number and manipulate them. You created only one subexpression, so its name is \1. A second subexpression would be \2, and so on, up to a maximum of \9. Your new filenames would have the form image\1.jpg. Therefore, your sed script would be:

```
$ ls | sed "s/image\.jpg\.\([1-3]\)/image\1.jpg/"
image1.jpg
image2.jpg
image3.jpg
```

To make things more complicated, suppose the filenames had more variation, consisting of lowercase words:

```
$ ls
apple.jpg.1  banana.png.2  carrot.jpg.3
```

Create three subexpressions to capture the base filename, extension, and final digit:

```
\([a-z][a-z]*\)        |1 = Base filename of one letter or more
\([a-z][a-z][a-z]\)    |2 = File extension of three letters
\([0-9]\)              |3 = A digit
```

Connect them with escaped dots (\.) to form this regular expression:

```
\([a-z][a-z]*\) \. \([a-z][a-z][a-z]\) \. \([0-9]\)
```

Represent the newly transformed filenames to sed as \1\3.\2, and the final substitution with sed becomes:

```
$ ls | sed "s/\([a-z][a-z]*\)\.\([a-z][a-z][a-z]\)\.\([0-9]\)/\1\3.\2/"
apple1.jpg
banana2.png
carrot3.jpg
```

This command does not rename files—it just prints the new names. The section "Inserting a Filename into a Sequence" on page 140 shows a similar example that performs the renaming as well.

To learn sed beyond what can be covered in a few book pages, take a sed tutorial at tutorialspoint.com/sed or grymoire.com/Unix/Sed.html or search the web for "sed tutorial."

Toward an Even Larger Toolbox

Most Linux systems come with thousands of command-line programs, and most of them have numerous options that change their behavior. You're not likely to learn and remember them all. So, in a moment of need, how do you locate a new program —or tailor a program that you already know—to accomplish your goals?

Your first (obvious) step is a web search engine. For example, if you need a command that limits the width of lines in a text file, wrapping any lines that are too long, search the web for (say) "Linux command wrap lines" and you'll be pointed to the fold command:

```
$ cat title.txt
This book is titled "Efficient Linux at the Command Line"
$ fold -w40 title.txt
This book is titled "Efficient Linux at
the Command Line"
```

To discover commands that are already installed on your Linux system, run the command man -k (or equivalently, apropos). Given a word, man -k searches for that word in the brief descriptions at the top of manpages:

```
$ man -k width
DisplayWidth (3)      - image format functions and macros
DisplayWidthMM (3)    - image format functions and macros
fold (1)              - wrap each input line to fit in specified width
⋮
```

man -k accepts awk-style regular expressions in search strings (see Table 5-1):

```
$ man -k "wide|width"
```

A command that's not installed on your system might still be installable through your system's package manager. A package manager is software for installing Linux programs that are supported for your system. Some popular package managers include apt, dnf, emerge, pacman, rpm, yum, and zypper. Use the man command to figure out which package manager is installed on your system and learn how to search for uninstalled packages. Often it's a two-command sequence: one command to copy the latest data about available packages ("metadata") from the internet onto your system, and another to search the metadata. For example, for Ubuntu or Debian Linux-based systems, the commands are:

```
$ sudo apt update              Download the latest metadata
$ apt-file search string       Search for a string
```

If, after much searching, you cannot locate or construct an appropriate command to meet your needs, consider asking for help in an online forum. A great starting point for asking effective questions is Stack Overflow's "How Do I Ask a Good Question?" help page (*https://oreil.ly/J0jho*). In general, present your questions in a way that is respectful of other people's time, and experts will be more inclined to answer. That means making your question short and to the point, including any error messages or other output word for word, and explaining what you have tried so far on your own. Spend quality time to ask a quality question: you'll not only increase your chances of a helpful answer, but also, if the forum is public and searchable, a clear question and answer may aid others who have a similar problem.

Summary

You've now grown beyond the pint-sized toolbox from Chapter 1 and are ready to tackle more challenging business problems at the command line. The coming chapters are filled with practical examples of using your new commands in all kinds of situations.

## CHAPTER 6

Parents, Children, and Environments

The purpose of the shell—to run commands—is so fundamental to Linux that you might think the shell is built into Linux in some special way. It is not. A shell is just an ordinary program like `ls` or `cat`. It is programmed to repeat the following steps over and over and over and over…

1. Print a prompt.
2. Read a command from stdin.
3. Evaluate and run the command.

Linux does a great job of hiding the fact that a shell is an ordinary program. When you log in, Linux automatically runs an instance of the shell for you, known as your *login shell*. It launches so seamlessly that it appears to *be* Linux, when really it's just a program launched on your behalf to interact with Linux.

 Where Is Your Login Shell?

If you log in at a nongraphical terminal, say, using an SSH client program, the login shell is the initial shell you interact with. It prints the first prompt and awaits your command.

Alternatively, if you're at the computer's console with a graphical display, your login shell runs behind the scenes. It launches a desktop environment such as GNOME, Unity, Cinnamon, or KDE Plasma. Then you can open terminal windows to run additional interactive shells.

The more you understand about the shell, the more effectively you can work with Linux and the fewer superstitions you'll develop about its inner workings. This chapter explores the following mysteries of shells more deeply than Chapter 2 did:

- Where shell programs are located

- How different shell instances may be related to each other

- Why different shell instances may have the same variables, values, aliases, and other context

- How to change a shell's default behavior by editing configuration files

By the end, I hope you'll find that these mysteries aren't so mysterious after all.

Shells Are Executable Files

The default shell on most Linux systems is bash,[1] and it's an ordinary program—an executable file—located in the system directory */bin* alongside cat, ls, grep, and other familiar commands:

```
$ cd /bin
$ ls -l bash cat ls grep
-rwxr-xr-x 1 root root 1113504 Jun  6  2019 bash
-rwxr-xr-x 1 root root   35064 Jan 18  2018 cat
-rwxr-xr-x 1 root root  219456 Sep 18  2019 grep
-rwxr-xr-x 1 root root  133792 Jan 18  2018 ls
```

bash is also not the only shell on your system, most likely. Valid shells are usually listed, one per line, in the file */etc/shells*:

```
$ cat /etc/shells
/bin/sh
/bin/bash
/bin/csh
/bin/zsh
```

To see which shell you're running, echo the shell variable SHELL:

```
$ echo $SHELL
/bin/bash
```

In theory, a Linux system can treat *any program* as a valid login shell, if a user account is configured to invoke it on login and it's listed in */etc/shells* (if required on your system). With superuser privileges, you can even write and install your own shell, like the script in Example 6-1. It reads any command and responds, "I'm sorry, I'm afraid I can't do that." This custom shell is intentionally silly, but it demonstrates that other programs can be just as legitimate a shell as */bin/bash*.

---

1 If you use a different shell, see also Appendix B.

Example 6-1. halshell: A shell that refuses to run your commands

```
#!/bin/bash
# Print a prompt
echo -n '$ '
# Read the user's input in a loop. Exit when the user presses Ctrl-D.
while read line; do
 # Ignore the input $line and print a message
 echo "I'm sorry, I'm afraid I can't do that"
 # Print the next prompt
 echo -n '$ '
done
```

Since bash is just a program, you can run it manually like any other command:

```
$ bash
```

If you do so, you'll just see another prompt, as if your command had no effect:

```
$
```

But really, you have run a new instance of bash. This new instance prints a prompt and awaits your command. To make the new instance more visible, change its prompt (say, to %%) by setting the shell variable PS1, and run some commands:

```
$ PS1="%% "
%% ls                              The prompt has changed
animals.txt
%% echo "This is a new shell"
This is a new shell
```

Now run exit to terminate the new instance of bash. You'll return to the original shell, which has a dollar-sign prompt:

```
%% exit
$
```

I must emphasize that the change from %% back to $ was not a prompt change. It was a whole shell change. The new instance of bash has ended, so the original shell prompts you for the next command.

Running bash by hand is not just for entertainment value. You'll use manually invoked shells to your advantage in Chapter 7.

Parent and Child Processes

When one instance of the shell invokes another, as I just demonstrated, the original shell is called the *parent* and the new instance is called the *child*. The same is true for any Linux program that invokes any other Linux program. The invoking program is the parent, and the invoked program is its child. A running Linux program is known as a *process*, so you'll also see the terms *parent process* and *child process*. A process can invoke any number of children, but each child has only one parent.

Every process has its own environment. An environment, which you might recall from "Environments and Initialization Files, the Short Version" on page 33, includes a current directory, search path, shell prompt, and other important information held in shell variables. When a child is created, its environment is largely a copy of its parent's environment. (I'll explain more in "Environment Variables" on page 99.)

Every time you run a simple command, you create a child process. This is such an important point for understanding Linux that I'll say it again: even when you run a simple command like ls, that command secretly runs inside a new child process with its own (copied) environment. That means any changes you make to a child, like changing the prompt variable PS1 in a child shell, affect only the child and are lost when the child exits. Likewise, any changes to the parent won't affect its children that are already running. Changes to the parent *can* affect its *future* children, however, because each child's environment is copied from its parent's environment on startup.

Why does it matter that commands run in child processes? For one thing, it means that any program you run can cd all over the filesystem, but when it exits, your current shell (the parent) has not changed its current directory. Here's a quick experiment to prove it. Create a shell script called cdtest in your home directory containing a cd command:

```
#!/bin/bash
cd /etc
echo "Here is my current directory:"
pwd
```

Make it executable:

```
$ chmod +x cdtest
```

Print your current directory name and then run the script:

```
$ pwd
/home/smith
$ ./cdtest
Here is my current directory:
/etc
```

Now check your current directory:

```
$ pwd
/home/smith
```

Your current directory hasn't changed, even though the cdtest script traveled to the */etc* directory. That's because cdtest ran inside a child process with its own environment. Changes to the child's environment cannot affect the parent's environment, so the parent's current directory did not change. The same thing happens when you run an executable program like cat or grep—it runs in a child process that exits after the program terminates, taking any environment changes with it.

Why cd Must Be a Shell Builtin

If Linux programs cannot change your shell's current directory, then how does the command cd manage to change it? Well, cd isn't a program. It's a built-in feature of the shell (a.k.a. a shell builtin). If cd were a program external to the shell, directory changes would be impossible—they would run in a child process and be unable to affect the original (parent) shell.

Pipelines launch multiple child processes: one for each command in the pipeline. This command from the section "Command #6: uniq" on page 14 launches six children:

```
$ cut -f1 grades | sort | uniq -c | sort -nr | head -n1 | cut -c9
```

Environment Variables

Every instance of the shell has a collection of variables, as you learned in "Evaluating Variables" on page 23. Some variables are local to a single shell. They are called *local variables*. Other variables are automatically copied from a given shell to each child it invokes. These variables are called *environment variables*, and they collectively form the shell's environment. Some examples of environment variables and their uses are:

HOME

The path to your home directory. Its value is set automatically by your login shell when you log in. Text editors like vim and emacs read the variable HOME so they can locate and read their configuration files (*$HOME/.vim* and *$HOME/.emacs*, respectively).

PWD

Your shell's current directory. Its value is set and maintained automatically by the shell each time you cd to another directory. The command pwd reads the variable PWD to print the name of your shell's current directory.

EDITOR

The name of (or path to) your preferred text editor. Its value is generally set by you in a shell configuration file. Other programs read this variable to launch an appropriate editor on your behalf.

View a shell's environment variables with the `printenv` command. The output is one variable per line, unsorted, and can be quite long, so pipe it though `sort` and `less` for friendlier viewing:[2]

```
$ printenv | sort -i | less
⋮
DISPLAY=:0
EDITOR=emacs
HOME=/home/smith
LANG=en_US.UTF-8
PWD=/home/smith/Music
SHELL=/bin/bash
TERM=xterm-256color
USER=smith
⋮
```

Local variables do not appear in the output of `printenv`. Display their values by preceding the variable name with a dollar sign and printing the result with `echo`:

```
$ title="Efficient Linux"
$ echo $title
Efficient Linux
$ printenv title                              (produces no output)
```

Creating Environment Variables

To turn a local variable into an environment variable, use the `export` command:

```
$ MY_VARIABLE=10                  A local variable
$ export MY_VARIABLE              Export it to become an environment variable
$ export ANOTHER_VARIABLE=20      Or, set and export in a single command
```

`export` specifies that the variable and its value will be copied from the current shell to any future children. Local variables are not copied to future children:

```
$ export E="I am an environment variable"     Set an environment variable
$ L="I am just a local variable"              Set a local variable
$ echo $E
I am an environment variable
$ echo $L
I am just a local variable
$ bash                                        Run a child shell
$ echo $E                                     Environment variable was copied
I am an environment variable
$ echo $L                                     Local variable was not copied
                                              Empty string is printed
$ exit                                        Exit the child shell
```

---

2 I have trimmed the output selectively to display common environment variables. Your output is likely much longer and full of obscure variable names.

Remember, a child's variables are *copies*. Any changes to the copy do not affect the parent shell:

```
$ export E="I am the original value"        Set an environment variable
$ bash                                      Run a child shell
$ echo $E
I am the original value                     Parent's value was copied
$ E="I was modified in a child"             Change the child's copy
$ echo $E
I was modified in a child
$ exit                                      Exit the child shell
$ echo $E
I am the original value                     Parent's value is unchanged
```

Launch a new shell anytime and change anything in its environment, and all the changes disappear when you exit the shell. This means you can experiment with shell features safely—just run a shell manually, creating a child, and terminate it when finished.

Superstition Alert: "Global" Variables

Sometimes Linux hides its inner workings too well. A great example is the behavior of environment variables. Somehow, like magic, variables like HOME and PATH each have a consistent value in all your shell instances. They seem to be "global variables" in some sense. (I've even seen this claim in other Linux books, not published by O'Reilly.) But an environment variable is *not global*. Each shell instance has its own copy. Modifying an environment variable in one shell cannot change the value in any other running shells. Modifications affect only that shell's future children (not yet invoked).

If that's the case, how does a variable like HOME or PATH seem to keep its value in all your shell instances? There are two avenues to make this happen, which are illustrated in Figure 6-1. In short:

Children copy from their parents.
> For variables like HOME, the values are usually set and exported by your login shell. All future shells (until you log out) are children of the login shell, so they receive a copy of the variable and its value. These sorts of system-defined environment variables are so rarely modified in the real world that they seem global, but they are just ordinary variables that play by the ordinary rules. (You may even change their values in a running shell, but you might disrupt the expected behavior of that shell and the programs it launches.)

Different instances read the same configuration files.
> Local variables, which are not copied to children, can have their values set in a Linux configuration file such as *$HOME/.bashrc* (see more details in "Configuring Your Environment" on page 103). Each instance of the shell, on invocation, reads and executes the appropriate configuration files. As a result, these local

variables appear to be copied from shell to shell. The same is true for other non-exported shell features such as aliases.

This behavior leads some users to believe that the export command creates a global variable. It does not. The command export WHATEVER simply declares that the variable WHATEVER will be copied from the current shell to any future children.

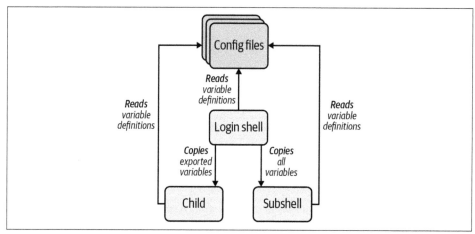

Figure 6-1. Shells may share variables and values by export or by reading the same configuration files

Child Shells Versus Subshells

A child is a partial copy of its parent. It includes copies of its parent's environment variables, for example, but not its parent's local (unexported) variables or aliases:

```
$ alias                         List aliases
alias gd='pushd'
alias l='ls -CF'
alias pd='popd'
$ bash --norc                   Run a child shell and ignore bashrc files
$ alias                         List aliases - none are known
$ echo $HOME                    Environment variables are known
/home/smith
$ exit                          Exit the child shell
```

If you've ever wondered why your aliases aren't available in shell scripts, now you know. Shell scripts run in a child, which does not receive copies of the parent's aliases.

A *subshell*, in contrast, is a complete copy of its parent.[3] It includes all the parent's variables, aliases, functions, and more. To launch a command in a subshell, enclose the command in parentheses:

```
$ (ls -l)                               Launches ls -l in a subshell
-rw-r--r-- 1 smith smith 325 Oct 13 22:19 animals.txt
$ (alias)                               View aliases in a subshell
alias gd=pushd
alias l=ls -CF
alias pd=popd
⋮
$ (l)                                   Run an alias from the parent
animals.txt
```

To check if a shell instance is a subshell, print the variable BASH_SUBSHELL. The value is nonzero in subshells, zero otherwise:

```
$ echo $BASH_SUBSHELL         Check the current shell
0                             Not a subshell
$ bash                        Run a child shell
$ echo $BASH_SUBSHELL         Check the child shell
0                             Not a subshell
$ exit                        Exit the child shell
$ (echo $BASH_SUBSHELL)       Run an explicit subshell
1                             Yes, it's a subshell
```

I'll cover some practical uses of subshells in "Technique #10: Explicit Subshells" on page 129. For now, just be aware that you can create them and they copy the parent's aliases.

Configuring Your Environment

When bash runs, it configures itself by reading a sequence of files, called *configuration files*, and executing their contents. These files define variables, aliases, functions, and other shell features, and they can include any Linux command. (They are like shell scripts that configure the shell.) Some configuration files are defined by the system administrator and apply to all users system-wide. They are found in the directory */etc*. Other configuration files are owned and changed by individual users. They are located in the user's home directory. Table 6-1 lists the standard bash configuration files. They come in several types:

---

3 It's complete except for traps, which "are reset to the values that the shell inherited from its parent at invocation" (man bash). I don't discuss traps further in this book.

Startup files

Configuration files that execute automatically when you log in—that is, they apply only to your login shell. An example command in this file might set and export an environment variable. Defining an alias in this file would be less helpful, however, because aliases are not copied to children.

Initialization ("init") files

Configuration files that execute for every shell instance that is not a login shell—for example, when you run an interactive shell by hand or a (noninteractive) shell script. An example initialization file command might set a variable or define an alias.

Cleanup files

Configuration files that execute immediately before your login shell exits. An example command in this file might be `clear` to blank your screen on logout.

Table 6-1. Standard configuration files sourced by bash

File type	Run by	System-wide location	Personal file locations (in order invoked)
Startup files	Login shells, on invocation	*/etc/profile*	*$HOME/.bash_profile*, *$HOME/.bash_login*, and *$HOME/.profile*
Init files	Interactive shells (nonlogin), on invocation	*/etc/bashrc* or */etc/bash.bashrc*, depending on distro (look in */etc* to check)	*$HOME/.bashrc*
	Shell scripts, on invocation	Set the variable BASH_ENV to the absolute path to an initialization file (example: `BASH_ENV=/usr/local/etc/bashrc`)	Set the variable BASH_ENV to the absolute path to an initialization file (example: `BASH_ENV=/usr/local/etc/bashrc`)
Cleanup files	Login shells, on exit	*/etc/bash.bash_logout*	*$HOME/.bash_logout*

Notice that you have three choices for personal startup files in your home directory (*.bash_profile*, *.bash_login*, and *.profile*). Most users can just pick one and stick with it. Your Linux distro probably supplies one of them already, prefilled with (ideally) useful commands. Things are a bit different if you happen to run other shells such as Bourne shell (*/bin/sh*) and Korn shell (*/bin/ksh*). These shells also read *.profile* and can fail if handed `bash`-specific commands to execute. Place `bash`-specific commands in *.bash_profile* or *.bash_login* instead (again, just pick one).

Users sometimes find the separation of personal startup files and the personal initialization file confusing. Why would you want your login shell to behave differently from other shells, say, that you open in multiple windows? The answer is, in many cases, you don't need them to behave differently. Your personal startup file might do little more than source your personal initialization file, *$HOME/.bashrc*, so all interactive shells (login or nonlogin) would have largely the same configuration.

In other cases, you might prefer to split responsibilities between your startup and initialization files. For example, your personal startup file might set and export your environment variables to be copied to future children, whereas *$HOME/.bashrc* might define all your aliases (which are not copied to children).

Another consideration is whether you log into a graphical, windowing desktop environment (GNOME, Unity, KDE Plasma, etc.) where your login shell may be hidden. In this case, you might not care how the login shell behaves because you interact only with its children, so you might put most or all of your configuration into *$HOME/.bashrc*.[4] On the other hand, if you primarily log in from a nongraphical terminal program such as an SSH client, then you directly interact with your login shell, so its configuration matters a lot.

In each of these cases, it's generally worthwhile to have your personal startup file source your personal initialization file:

```
# Place in $HOME/.bash_profile or other personal startup file
if [ -f "$HOME/.bashrc" ]
then
   source "$HOME/.bashrc"
fi
```

Whatever you do, try not to place identical configuration commands in two different configuration files. That's a recipe for confusion, and it's hard to maintain, because any change you make to one file you must remember to duplicate in the other (and you'll forget, trust me). Instead, source one file from the other as I've shown.

Rereading a Configuration File

When you change any startup or initialization file, you can force a running shell to reread it by sourcing the file, as explained in "Environments and Initialization Files, the Short Version" on page 33:

```
$ source ~/.bash_profile        Uses the builtin "source" command
$ . ~/.bash_profile             Uses a dot
```

Why the source Command Exists

Why do you source a configuration file instead of making it executable with `chmod` and running it like a shell script? Because a script runs in a child process. Any commands in the script would not affect your intended (parent) shell. They would affect only the child, which exits, leaving you with nothing changed.

---

4 To make matters slightly more confusing, some desktop environments have their own shell configuration files. For example, GNOME has *$HOME/.gnomerc*, and the underlying X window system has *$HOME/.xinitrc*.

Traveling with Your Environment

If you use many Linux machines in multiple locations, at some point you might want to install your carefully crafted configuration files on more than one machine. Don't copy individual files from machine to machine—that approach leads to confusion eventually. Instead, store and maintain the files in a free account on GitHub (*https://github.com*) or a similar software-development service with version control. Then you can download, install, and update your configuration files conveniently and consistently on any Linux machine. If you make a mistake editing a configuration file, you can roll back to a previous version by issuing a command or two. Version control is beyond the scope of this book; see "Apply Version Control to Day-to-Day Files" on page 197 to learn more about it.

If you aren't comfortable with version control systems like Git or Subversion, store the configuration files on a simple file service like Dropbox, Google Drive, or One-Drive. Updates to your configuration files will be less convenient, but at least the files will be easily available for copying to other Linux systems.

Summary

I have met many Linux users who are puzzled by (or unaware of) parent and child processes, environments, and the purposes of the many shell configuration files. After reading this chapter, I hope you have a clearer picture of all these things. They come into play in Chapter 7 as powerful tools for running commands in flexible ways.

11 More Ways to Run a Command

Now that you have lots of commands in your toolbox and a thorough understanding of the shell, it's time to learn... how to run commands. Wait a minute, haven't you been running commands since the beginning of the book? Well, yes, but only in two ways. The first is the ordinary execution of a simple command:

```
$ grep Nutshell animals.txt
```

The second is a pipeline of simple commands, as covered in Chapter 1:

```
$ cut -f1 grades | sort | uniq -c | sort -nr
```

In this chapter, I'll show you 11 more ways to run a command and why you should care to learn them. Each technique has pros and cons, and the more techniques you know, the more flexibly and efficiently you can interact with Linux. I'll stick to the basics of each technique for now; you'll see more intricate examples in the next two chapters.

List Techniques

A list is a sequence of commands on a single command line. You've already seen one type of list—a pipeline—but the shell supports others with different behavior:

Conditional lists
    Each command depends on the success or failure of the previous one.

Unconditional lists
    Commands simply run one after the other.

Technique #1: Conditional Lists

Suppose you want to create a file *new.txt* in a directory *dir*. A typical sequence of commands might be:

```
$ cd dir          Enter the directory
$ touch new.txt   Make the file
```

Notice how the second command depends on the success of the first. If the directory *dir* doesn't exist, there is no point in running the touch command. The shell lets you make this dependency explicit. If you place the operator && (pronounced "and") between the two commands on a single line:

```
$ cd dir && touch new.txt
```

then the second command (touch) runs only if the first command (cd) succeeds. The preceding example is a *conditional list* of two commands. (To learn what it means for a command to "succeed," see "Exit Codes Indicate Success or Failure" on page 109.)

Very likely, you run commands every day that depend on previous ones. For example, have you ever made a backup copy of a file for safekeeping, modified the original, and deleted the backup when done?

```
$ cp myfile.txt myfile.safe   Make a backup copy
$ nano myfile.txt             Change the original
$ rm myfile.safe              Delete the backup
```

Each of these commands makes sense only if the preceding command succeeds. Therefore, this sequence is a candidate for a conditional list:

```
$ cp myfile.txt myfile.safe && nano myfile.txt && rm myfile.safe
```

As another example, if you use the version-control system Git to maintain files, you're probably familiar with the following sequence of commands after you change some files: run git add to prepare files for a commit, then git commit, and finally git push to share your committed changes. If any of these commands failed, you wouldn't run the rest (until you fixed the cause of the failure). Therefore, these three commands work well as a conditional list:

```
$ git add . && git commit -m"fixed a bug" && git push
```

Just as the && operator runs a second command only if the first succeeds, the related operator || (pronounced "or") runs a second command only if the first fails. For example, the following command tries to enter *dir*, and if it fails to do so, it creates *dir*:[1]

---

1 The command mkdir -p dir, which creates a directory path only if it doesn't already exist, would be a more elegant solution here.

```
$ cd dir || mkdir dir
```

You'll commonly see the || operator in scripts, causing the script to exit if an error occurs:

```
# If a directory can't be entered, exit with an error code of 1
cd dir || exit 1
```

Combine the && and || operators to set up more complicated actions for success and failure. The following command tries to enter directory *dir*, and if it fails, it creates the directory and enters it. If all fails, the command prints a failure message:

```
$ cd dir || mkdir dir && cd dir || echo "I failed"
```

The commands in a conditional list don't have to be simple commands; they can also be pipelines and other combined commands.

Exit Codes Indicate Success or Failure

What does it mean for a Linux command to succeed or fail? Every Linux command produces a result when it terminates, called an *exit code*. By convention, an exit code of zero means success and any nonzero value means failure.[2] View the exit code of a shell's most recently completed command by printing the special shell variable whose name is a question mark (?):

```
$ ls myfile.txt
myfile.txt
$ echo $?                        Print the value of the ? variable
0                                ls succeeded
$ cp nonexistent.txt somewhere.txt
cp: cannot stat 'nonexistent.txt': No such file or directory
$ echo $?
1                                cp failed
```

Technique #2: Unconditional Lists

Commands in a list don't have to depend on one another. If you separate the commands with semicolons, they simply run in order. Success or failure of a command does not affect later ones in the list.

I like unconditional lists for launching ad hoc commands after I've left work for the day. Here's one that sleeps (does nothing) for two hours (7,200 seconds) and then backs up my important files:

```
$ sleep 7200; cp -a ~/important-files /mnt/backup_drive
```

---

2 This behavior is opposite of what many programming languages do, where zero means failure.

Here's a similar command that functions as a primitive reminder system, sleeping for five minutes and then sending me an email:[3]

```
$ sleep 300; echo "remember to walk the dog" | mail -s reminder $USER
```

Unconditional lists are a convenience feature: they produce the same results (mostly) as typing the commands individually and pressing Enter after each. The only significant difference relates to exit codes. In an unconditional list, the exit codes of the individual commands are thrown away except the last one. Only the exit code of the last command run in the list is assigned to the shell variable ?:

```
$ mv file1 file2; mv file2 file3; mv file3 file4
$ echo $?
0                          The exit code for "mv file3 file4"
```

Substitution Techniques

Substitution means automatically replacing the text of a command with other text. I'll show you two types with powerful possibilities:

Command substitution
    A command is replaced by its output.

Process substitution
    A command is replaced by a file (sort of).

Technique #3: Command Substitution

Suppose you have a few thousand text files representing songs. Each file includes a song title, artist name, album title, and the song lyrics:

```
Title: Carry On Wayward Son
Artist: Kansas
Album: Leftoverture

Carry on my wayward son
There'll be peace when you are done
⋮
```

You'd like to organize the files into subdirectories by artist. To perform this task by hand, you could search for all song files by Kansas using grep:

```
$ grep -l "Artist: Kansas" *.txt
carry_on_wayward_son.txt
dust_in_the_wind.txt
belexes.txt
```

---

3 Alternatively, you could use cron for the backup job and at for reminders, but Linux is all about flexibility—finding multiple ways to achieve the same result.

---

and then move each file to a directory *kansas*:

```
$ mkdir kansas
$ mv carry_on_wayward_son.txt kansas
$ mv dust_in_the_wind.txt kansas
$ mv belexes.txt kansas
```

Tedious, right? Wouldn't be great if you could tell the shell, "Move all files that contain the string *Artist: Kansas* to the directory *kansas*." In Linux terms, you'd like to take the list of names from the preceding grep -l command and hand it to mv. Well, you can do this easily with the help of a shell feature called *command substitution*:

```
$ mv $(grep -l "Artist: Kansas" *.txt) kansas
```

The syntax:

```
$(any command here)
```

executes the command inside the parentheses and replaces the command by its output. So on the preceding command line, the grep -l command is replaced by the list of filenames that it prints, as if you had typed the filenames like this:

```
$ mv carry_on_wayward_son.txt dust_in_the_wind.txt belexes.txt kansas
```

Whenever you find yourself copying the output of one command into a later command line, you can usually save time with command substitution. You can even include aliases in command substitution, because its contents are run in a subshell, which includes copies of its parent's aliases.

Special Characters and Command Substitution

The preceding example with grep -l works great for most Linux filenames, but not for filenames that contain spaces or other special characters. The shell evaluates these characters before the output is handed to mv, potentially producing unexpected results. For example, if grep -l printed *dust in the wind.txt*, the shell would treat the spaces as separators, and mv would attempt to move four nonexistent files named *dust*, *in*, *the*, and *wind.txt*.

Here's another example. Suppose you have several years' worth of bank statements downloaded in PDF format. The downloaded files have names that include the statement's year, month, and day, such as *eStmt_2021-08-26.pdf* for the date August 26, 2021.[4] You'd like to view the most recent statement in the current directory. You could do it manually: list the directory, locate the file with the most recent date (which will be the final file in the listing), and display it with a Linux PDF viewer such as okular.

---

4 Bank of America's downloadable statement files are named this way at press time.

But why do all that manual work? Let command substitution ease your way. Create a command that prints the name of the latest PDF file in the directory:

```
$ ls eStmt*pdf | tail -n1
```

and provide it to okular using command substitution:

```
$ okular $(ls eStmt*pdf | tail -n1)
```

The `ls` command lists all the statement files, and `tail` prints only the last one, such as *eStmt_2021-08-26.pdf*. Command substitution places that single filename right onto the command line, as if you'd typed `okular eStmt-2021-08-26.pdf`.

The original syntax for command substitution was backquotes (backticks). The following two commands are equivalent:

```
$ echo Today is $(date +%A).
Today is Saturday.
$ echo Today is `date +%A`.
Today is Saturday.
```

Backticks are supported by most shells. The `$()` syntax is simpler to nest, however:

```
$ echo $(date +%A) | tr a-z A-Z                    Single
SATURDAY
echo Today is $( echo $(date +%A) | tr a-z A-Z )!   Nested
Today is SATURDAY!
```

In scripts, a common use of command substitution is to store the output of a command in a variable:

```
VariableName=$(some command here)
```

For example, to get the filenames containing Kansas songs and store them in a variable, use command substitution like so:

```
$ kansasFiles=$(grep -l "Artist: Kansas" *.txt)
```

The output might have multiple lines, so to preserve any newline characters, make sure you quote the value wherever you use it:

```
$ echo "$kansasFiles"
```

Technique #4: Process Substitution

Command substitution, which you just saw, replaces a command with its output in place, as a string. *Process substitution* also replaces a command with its output, but it treats the output as if it were stored in a file. This powerful difference may look confusing at first, so I'll explain it step-by-step.

Suppose you're in a directory of JPEG image files named *1.jpg* through *1000.jpg*, but some files are mysteriously missing and you want to identify them. Produce such a directory with the following commands:

```
$ mkdir /tmp/jpegs && cd /tmp/jpegs
$ touch {1..1000}.jpg
$ rm 4.jpg 981.jpg
```

A poor way to locate the missing files is to list the directory, sorted numerically, and look for gaps by eye:

```
$ ls -1 | sort -n | less
1.jpg
2.jpg
3.jpg
5.jpg          4.jpg is missing
:
```

A more robust, automated solution is to compare the existing filenames to a complete list of names from *1.jpg* to *1000.jpg*, using the diff command. One way to achieve this solution is with temporary files. Store the existing filenames, sorted, in one temporary file, *original-list*:

```
$ ls *.jpg | sort -n > /tmp/original-list
```

Then print a complete list of filenames from *1.jpg* to *1000.jpg* to another temporary file, *full-list*, by generating the integers 1 to 1000 with seq, and appending ".jpg" to each line with sed:

```
$ seq 1 1000 | sed 's/$/.jpg/' > /tmp/full-list
```

Compare the two temporary files with the diff command to discover that *4.jpg* and *981.jpg* are missing, then delete the temporary files:

```
$ diff /tmp/original-list /tmp/full-list
3a4
> 4.jpg
979a981
> 981.jpg
$ rm /tmp/original-list /tmp/full-list          Clean up afterwards
```

That's a lot of steps. Wouldn't it be grand to compare the two lists of names directly and not bother with temporary files? The challenge is that diff can't compare two lists from stdin; it requires files as arguments.[5] Process substitution solves the problem. It makes both lists appear to diff as files. (The sidebar "How Process Substitution Works" on page 115 provides the technical details.) The syntax:

```
<(any command here)
```

---

[5] Technically, diff can read one list from stdin if you provide a dash as a filename, but not two lists.

runs the command in a subshell and presents its output as if it were contained in a file. For example, the following expression represents the output of `ls -1 | sort -n` as if it were contained in a file:

```
<(ls -1 | sort -n)
```

You can cat the file:

```
$ cat <(ls -1 | sort -n)
1.jpg
2.jpg
⋮
```

You can copy the file with `cp`:

```
$ cp <(ls -1 | sort -n) /tmp/listing
$ cat /tmp/listing
1.jpg
2.jpg
⋮
```

and as you'll now see, you can `diff` the file against another. Begin with the two commands that generated your two temporary files:

```
ls *.jpg | sort -n
seq 1 1000 | sed 's/$/.jpg/'
```

Apply process substitution so `diff` can treat them as files, and you get the same output as before, but without using temporary files:

```
$ diff <(ls *.jpg | sort -n) <(seq 1 1000 | sed 's/$/.jpg/')
3a4
> 4.jpg
979a981
> 981.jpg
```

Clean up the output by grepping for lines beginning with > and stripping off the first two characters with `cut`, and you have your missing files report:

```
$ diff <(ls *.jpg | sort -n) <(seq 1 1000 | sed 's/$/.jpg/') \
    | grep '>' \
    | cut -c3-
4.jpg
981.jpg
```

Process substitution transformed how I use the command line. Commands that read only from disk files suddenly could read from stdin. With practice, commands that previously seemed impossible became easy.

Command-as-String Techniques

Every command is a string, but some commands are more "stringy" than others. I'll show you several techniques that construct a string, piece by piece, and then run the string as a command:

- Passing a command to bash as an argument
- Piping commands to bash on stdin
- Sending commands to another host with ssh
- Running a sequence of commands with xargs

 The following techniques can be risky because they send unseen text to a shell for execution. Never do this blindly. Always understand the text (and trust its origin) before executing it. You don't want to execute the string "rm -rf $HOME" by mistake and wipe out all your files.

Technique #5: Passing a Command as an Argument to bash

bash is a normal command like any other, as explained in "Shells Are Executable Files" on page 96, so you can run it by name on the command line. By default, running bash launches an interactive shell for typing and executing commands, as you've seen. Alternatively, you can pass a command to bash as a string, via the -c option, and bash will run that string as a command and exit:

```
$ bash -c "ls -l"
-rw-r--r-- 1 smith smith 325 Jul  3 17:44 animals.txt
```

Why is this helpful? Because the new bash process is a child with its own environment, including a current directory, variables with values, and so on. Any changes to the child shell won't affect your currently running shell. Here's a bash -c command that changes directory to */tmp* just long enough to delete a file, then exits:

```
$ pwd
/home/smith
$ touch /tmp/badfile                      Create a temporary file
$ bash -c "cd /tmp && rm badfile"
$ pwd
/home/smith                               Current directory is unchanged
```

The most instructive and beautiful use of bash -c, however, arises when you run certain commands as the superuser. Specifically, the combination of sudo and input/output redirection produces an interesting (sometimes maddening) situation in which bash -c is the key to success.

Suppose you want to create a log file in the system directory */var/log*, which is not writable by ordinary users. You run the following sudo command to gain superuser privileges and create the log file, but it mysteriously fails:

```
$ sudo echo "New log file" > /var/log/custom.log
bash: /var/log/custom.log: Permission denied
```

Wait a minute—sudo should give you permission to create any file anywhere. How can this command possibly fail? Why didn't sudo even prompt you for a password? The answer is: because sudo didn't run. You applied sudo to the echo command but not to the output redirection, which ran first and failed. In detail:

1. You pressed Enter.
2. The shell began to evaluate the whole command, including redirection (>).
3. The shell tried to create the file *custom.log* in a protected directory, */var/log*.
4. You didn't have permission to write to */var/log*, so the shell gave up and printed the "Permission denied" message.

That's why sudo never ran. To solve this problem, you need to tell the shell, "Run the entire command, including output redirection, as the superuser." This is exactly the kind of situation that bash -c solves so well. Construct the command you want to run, as a string:

```
'echo "New log file" > /var/log/custom.log'
```

and pass it as an argument to sudo bash -c:

```
$ sudo bash -c 'echo "New log file" > /var/log/custom.log'
[sudo] password for smith: xxxxxxxx
$ cat /var/log/custom.log
New log file
```

This time, you've run bash, not just echo, as the superuser, and bash executes the entire string as a command. The redirection succeeds. Remember this technique whenever you pair sudo with redirection.

Technique #6: Piping a Command to bash

The shell reads every command that you type on stdin. That means bash the program can participate in pipelines. For example, print the string "ls -l" and pipe it to bash, and bash will treat the string as a command and run it:

```
$ echo "ls -l"
ls -l
$ echo "ls -l" | bash
-rw-r--r-- 1 smith smith 325 Jul  3 17:44 animals.txt
```

Remember, never blindly pipe text to bash. Be aware of what you're executing.

This technique is terrific when you need to run many similar commands in a row. If you can print the commands as strings, then you can pipe the strings to bash for execution. Suppose you're in a directory with many files, and you want to organize them into subdirectories by their first character. A file named *apple* would be moved to subdirectory *a*, a file named *cantaloupe* would move to subdirectory *c*, and so on.[6] (For simplicity, we'll assume all the filenames begin with a lowercase letter and contain no spaces or special characters.)

---

6 This directory structure is similar to a hashtable with chaining.

First, list the files, sorted. We'll assume all the names are at least two characters long (matching the pattern ??*) so our commands don't collide with the subdirectories *a* through *z*:

```
$ ls -1 ??*
apple
banana
cantaloupe
carrot
⋮
```

Create the 26 subdirectories you need via brace expansion:

```
$ mkdir {a..z}
```

Now generate the mv commands you'll need, as strings. Start with a regular expression for sed that captures the first character of the filename as expression #1 (\1):

```
^\(.\)
```

Capture the rest of the filename as expression #2 (\2):

```
\(.*\)$
```

Connect the two regular expressions:

```
^\(.\)\(.*\)$
```

Now form a mv command with the word *mv* followed by a space, the full filename (\1\2), another space, and the first character (\1):

```
mv \1\2 \1
```

The complete command generator is:

```
$ ls -1 ??* | sed 's/^\(.\)\(.*\)$/mv \1\2 \1/'
mv apple a
mv banana b
mv cantaloupe c
mv carrot c
⋮
```

Its output contains exactly the mv commands you need. Read the output to convince yourself it's correct, perhaps by piping it to less for page-by-page viewing:

```
$ ls -1 ??* | sed 's/^\(.\)\(.*\)$/mv \1\2 \1/' | less
```

When you're satisfied that your generated commands are correct, pipe the output to bash for execution:

```
$ ls -1 ??* | sed 's/^\(.\)\(.*\)$/mv \1\2 \1/' | bash
```

The steps you just completed are a repeatable pattern:

1. Print a sequence of commands by manipulating strings.

2. View the results with `less` to check correctness.

3. Pipe the results to `bash`.

Technique #7: Executing a String Remotely with ssh

Disclaimer: this technique will make sense only if you're familiar with SSH, the secure shell, for logging into remote hosts. Setting up SSH relationships between hosts is beyond the scope of this book; to learn more about it, seek out an SSH tutorial.

In addition to the usual way of logging into a remote host:

```
$ ssh myhost.example.com
```

you also can execute a single command on the remote host—by passing a string to ssh on the command line. Simply append the string to the rest of the `ssh` command line:

```
$ ssh myhost.example.com ls
remotefile1
remotefile2
remotefile3
```

This technique is generally quicker than logging in, running a command, and logging out. If the command includes special characters, such as redirection symbols, that need to be evaluated on the remote host, then quote or escape them. Otherwise, they'll be evaluated by your local shell. Both of the following commands run `ls` remotely, but the output redirection occurs on different hosts:

```
$ ssh myhost.example.com ls > outfile        Creates outfile on local host
$ ssh myhost.example.com "ls > outfile"      Creates outfile on remote host
```

You can also pipe commands to ssh to run them on the remote host, much like you pipe them to bash to run locally:

```
$ echo "ls > outfile" | ssh myhost.example.com
```

When piping commands to ssh, the remote host might print diagnostic or other messages. These generally do not affect the remote command, and you can suppress them:

- If you see messages about pseudo-terminals or pseudo-ttys, such as "Pseudo-terminal will not be allocated because stdin is not a terminal," run ssh with the -T option to prevent the remote SSH server from allocating a terminal:

```
$ echo "ls > outfile" | ssh -T myhost.example.com
```

- If you see welcome messages that normally appear when you log in ("Welcome to Linux!") or other unwanted messages, try telling ssh explicitly to run bash on the remote host, and the messages should disappear:

```
$ echo "ls > outfile" | ssh myhost.example.com bash
```

Technique #8: Running a List of Commands with xargs

Many Linux users have never heard of the command xargs, but it's a powerful tool for constructing and running multiple, similar commands. Learning xargs was another transformative moment in my Linux education, and I hope yours as well.

xargs accepts two inputs:

- On stdin: A list of strings separated by whitespace. An example is file paths produced by ls or find, but any strings will do. I'll call them the *input strings*.

- On the command line: An incomplete command that's missing some arguments, which I'll call the *command template*.

xargs merges the input strings and the command template to produce and run new, complete commands, which I'll call the *generated commands*. I'll demonstrate this process with a toy example. Suppose you're in a directory with three files:

```
$ ls -1
apple
banana
cantaloupe
```

Pipe the directory listing to xargs to serve as its input strings, and provide wc -l to serve as the command template, like so:

```
$ ls -1 | xargs wc -l
3 apple
4 banana
1 cantaloupe
8 total
```

As promised, xargs applied the wc -l command template to the input strings and counts lines in each file. To print the same three files with cat, simply change the command template to "cat":

```
$ ls -1 | xargs cat
```

My toy examples with xargs have two shortcomings, one fatal and one practical. The fatal shortcoming is that xargs may do the wrong thing if an input string contains special characters, such as spaces. A robust solution is in the sidebar "Safety with find and xargs" on page 122.

The practical shortcoming is that you don't need xargs here—you can accomplish the same tasks more simply with file pattern matching:

```
$ wc -l *
3 apple
4 banana
1 cantaloupe
8 total
```

Why use xargs, then? Its power becomes apparent when the input strings are more interesting than a simple directory listing. Suppose you want to count lines in all files in a directory *and all its subdirectories* (recursively), but only for Python source files with names ending in *.py*. It's easy to produce such a list of file paths with find:

```
$ find . -type f -name \*.py -print
fruits/raspberry.py
vegetables/leafy/lettuce.py
⋮
```

xargs can now apply the command template wc -l to each file path, producing a recursive result that would be difficult to obtain otherwise. For safety, I'll replace the option -print with -print0, and xargs with xargs -0, for reasons explained in the sidebar "Safety with find and xargs" on page 122:

```
$ find . -type f -name \*.py -print0 | xargs -0 wc -l
6 ./fruits/raspberry.py
3 ./vegetables/leafy/lettuce.py
⋮
```

By combining find and xargs, you can empower any command to run recursively through the filesystem, affecting only files (and/or directories) that match your stated criteria. (In some cases, you can produce the same effect with find alone, using its option -exec, but xargs is often a cleaner solution.)

xargs has numerous options (see man xargs) that control how it creates and runs the generated commands. The most important ones in my view (other than -0) are -n and -I. The -n option controls how many arguments are appended by xargs onto each generated command. The default behavior is to append as many arguments as will fit within the shell's limits:[7]

---

7 The exact number depends on length limits on your Linux system; see man xargs.

```
$ ls | xargs echo              Fit as many input strings as possible:
apple banana cantaloupe carrot    echo apple banana cantaloupe carrot
$ ls | xargs -n1 echo          One argument per echo command:
apple                             echo apple
banana                            echo banana
cantaloupe                        echo cantaloupe
carrot                            echo carrot
$ ls | xargs -n2 echo          Two arguments per echo command:
apple banana                      echo apple banana
cantaloupe carrot                 echo cantaloupe carrot
$ ls | xargs -n3 echo          Three arguments per echo command:
apple banana cantaloupe           echo apple banana cantaloupe
carrot                            echo carrot
```

Safety with find and xargs

When combining find and xargs, use xargs -0 (dash zero) rather than xargs alone to protect against unexpected special characters in the input strings. Pair it with the output produced by find -print0 (instead of find -print):

```
$ find options... -print0 | xargs -0 options...
```

Normally, xargs expects its input strings to be separated by whitespace, such as newline characters. This is a problem when the input strings themselves contain other whitespace, such as filenames with spaces in them. By default, xargs will treat those spaces as input separators and operate on incomplete strings, producing incorrect results. For example, if the input to xargs includes a line *prickly pear.py*, xargs will treat it as two input strings, and you're likely to see an error like this:

```
prickly: No such file or directory
pear.py: No such file or directory
```

To avoid this problem, use xargs -0 (that's a zero) to accept a different character as the input separator, namely, the null character (ASCII zero). Nulls rarely appear in text, so they are ideal, unambiguous separators for input strings.

How can you separate your input strings with nulls instead of newlines? Fortunately, find has an option to do exactly that: -print0, rather than -print.

The ls command unfortunately does not have an option to separate its output with nulls, so my earlier toy examples with ls are not safe. You can convert newlines to nulls with tr:

```
$ ls | tr '\n' '\0' | xargs -0 ...
```

Or use this handy alias that lists the current directory with entries separated by nulls, suitable for piping to xargs:

```
alias ls0="find . -maxdepth 1 -print0"
```

The -I option controls where the input strings appear in the generated command. By default, they're appended to the command template, but you can make them appear elsewhere. Follow -I with any string (of your choice), and that string becomes a placeholder in the command template, indicating exactly where input strings should be inserted:

```
$ ls | xargs -I XYZ echo XYZ is my favorite food      Use XYZ as a placeholder
apple is my favorite food
banana is my favorite food
cantaloupe is my favorite food
carrot is my favorite food
```

I chose "XYZ" arbitrarily as a placeholder for input strings and positioned it immediately after echo, moving the input string to the beginning of each output line. Note that the -I option limits xargs to one input string per generated command. I recommend reading the xargs manpage thoroughly to learn what else you can control.

Long Argument Lists

xargs is a problem solver when command lines grow very long. Suppose your current directory contains one million files named *file1.txt* through *file1000000.txt* and you try to remove them by pattern matching:

```
$ rm *.txt
bash: /bin/rm: Argument list too long
```

The pattern *.txt evaluates to a string of more than 14 million characters, which is longer than Linux supports. To work around this limitation, pipe a list of the files to xargs for deletion. xargs will split the list of files across multiple rm commands. Form the list of files by piping a full directory listing to grep, matching only filenames ending in *.txt*, then pipe to xargs:

```
$ ls | grep '\.txt$' | xargs rm
```

This solution is better than file pattern matching (ls *.txt), which will produce the same "Argument list too long" error. Better yet, run find -print0 as described in "Safety with find and xargs" on page 122:

```
$ find . -maxdepth 1 -name \*.txt -type f -print0 \
  | xargs -0 rm
```

Process-Control Techniques

So far, all commands I've discussed occupy the parent shell until they finish. Let's consider several techniques that forge a different relationship with the parent shell:

Background commands
   Immediately return the prompt and execute out of sight

Explicit subshells
   Can be launched in the middle of a combined command

Process replacement
   Supersedes the parent shell

Technique #9: Backgrounding a Command

So far, all our techniques run a command to completion while you wait, and then present the next shell prompt. But you don't have to wait, especially for commands that take a long time. You can launch commands in a special way so they disappear from sight (sort of) yet continue to run, freeing up the current shell immediately to run further commands. This technique is called *backgrounding* a command or *running a command in the background*. In contrast, commands that occupy the shell are called *foreground* commands. A shell instance runs at most one foreground command at a time plus any number of background commands.

Launching a command in the background

To run a command in the background, simply append an ampersand (&). The shell responds with a cryptic-looking message indicating that the command is backgrounded and presents the next prompt:

```
$ wc -c my_extremely_huge_file.txt &      Count characters in a huge file
[1] 74931                                 Cryptic-looking response
$
```

You can then continue running foreground commands (or more background commands) in this shell. Output from backgrounded commands may appear at any time, even while you are typing. If the backgrounded command finishes successfully, the shell will inform you with a *Done* message:

```
59837483748 my_extremely_huge_file.txt
[1]+  Done                    wc -c my_extremely_huge_file.txt
```

or if it fails, you'll see an *Exit* message with an exit code:

```
[1]+  Exit 1                  wc -c my_extremely_huge_file.txt
```

The ampersand is also a list operator, like && and ||:

```
$ command1 & command2 & command3 &     All 3 commands
[1] 57351                               in background
[2] 57352
[3] 57353
$ command4 & command5 & echo hi         All in background
[1] 57431                               but "echo"
[2] 57432
hi
```

Suspending a command and sending it to the background

A related technique is to run a foreground command, change your mind during execution, and send it to the background. Press Ctrl-Z to stop the command temporarily (called *suspending* the command) and return to the shell prompt; then type bg to resume running the command in the background.

Jobs and job control

Background commands are part of a shell feature called *job control* that manipulates running commands in various ways, like backgrounding, suspending, and resuming them. A *job* is a shell's unit of work: a single instance of a command running in a shell. Simple commands, pipelines, and conditional lists are all examples of jobs— basically anything you can run at the command line.

A job is more than a Linux process. A job may consist of one process, two processes, or more. A pipeline of six programs, for example, is a single job that includes (at least) six processes. Jobs are a construct of the shell. The Linux operating system doesn't keep track of jobs, just the underlying processes.

At any moment, a shell may have multiple jobs running. Each job in a given shell has a positive integer ID, called the job ID or job number. When you run a command in the background, the shell prints the job number and the ID of the first process it runs within the job. In the following command, the job number is 1 and the process ID is 74931:

```
$ wc -c my_extremely_huge_file.txt &
[1] 74931
```

Common job-control operations

The shell has built-in commands for controlling jobs, listed in Table 7-1. I'll demonstrate the most common job-control operations by running a bunch of jobs and manipulating them. To keep the jobs simple and predictable, I'll run the command sleep, which just sits there doing nothing ("sleeping") for a given number of seconds and then exits. For example, sleep 10 sleeps for 10 seconds.

Table 7-1. Job control commands

Command	Meaning
bg	Move the current suspended job into the background
bg %*n*	Move suspended job number *n* into the background (example: bg %1)
fg	Move the current background job into the foreground
fg %*n*	Move background job number *n* into the foreground (example: fg %2)
kill %*n*	Terminate background job number *n* (example: kill %3)
jobs	View a shell's jobs

Run a job in the background to completion:

```
$ sleep 20 &                    Run in the background
[1] 126288
$ jobs                          List this shell's jobs
[1]+  Running        sleep 20 &
$
...eventually...
[1]+  Done           sleep 20
```

When jobs complete, the *Done* message might not appear until the next time you press Enter.

Run a background job and bring it into the foreground:

```
$ sleep 20 &                    Run in the background
[1] 126362
$ fg                            Bring into the foreground
sleep 20
...eventually...
$
```

Run a foreground job, suspend it, and bring it back into the foreground:

```
$ sleep 20                      Run in the foreground
^Z                              Suspend the job
[1]+  Stopped        sleep 20
$ jobs                          List this shell's jobs
[1]+  Stopped        sleep 20
$ fg                            Bring into the foreground
sleep 20
...eventually...
[1]+  Done           sleep 20
```

Run a foreground job and send it to the background:

```
$ sleep 20                              Run in the foreground
^Z                                      Suspend the job
[1]+  Stopped          sleep 20
$ bg                                    Move to the background
[1]+ sleep 20 &
$ jobs                                  List this shell's jobs
[1]+  Running          sleep 20 &
$
...eventually...
[1]+  Done             sleep 20
```

Work with multiple background jobs. Refer to a job by its job number preceded by a percent sign (%1, %2, and so on):

```
$ sleep 100 &                           Run 3 commands in the background
[1] 126452
$ sleep 200 &
[2] 126456
$ sleep 300 &
[3] 126460
$ jobs                                  List this shell's jobs
[1]   Running          sleep 100 &
[2]-  Running          sleep 200 &
[3]+  Running          sleep 300 &
$ fg %2                                 Bring job 2 into the foreground
sleep 200
^Z                                      Suspend job 2
[2]+  Stopped          sleep 200
$ jobs                                  See job 2 is suspended ("stopped")
[1]   Running          sleep 100 &
[2]+  Stopped          sleep 200
[3]-  Running          sleep 300 &
$ kill %3                               Terminate job 3
[3]+  Terminated       sleep 300
$ jobs                                  See job 3 is gone
[1]-  Running          sleep 100 &
[2]+  Stopped          sleep 200
$ bg %2                                 Resume suspended job 2 in the background
[2]+ sleep 200 &
$ jobs                                  See job 2 is running again
[1]-  Running          sleep 100 &
[2]+  Running          sleep 200 &
$
```

Output and input in the background

A backgrounded command may write to stdout, sometimes at inconvenient or confusing times. Notice what happens if you sort the Linux dictionary file (100,000 lines long) and print the first two lines in the background. As expected, the shell immediately prints the job number (1), a process ID (81089), and the next prompt:

```
$ sort /usr/share/dict/words | head -n2 &
[1] 81089
$
```

If you wait until the job finishes, it prints two lines on stdout wherever your cursor happens to be at the time. In this case, the cursor is sitting at the second prompt, so you get this sloppy-looking output:

```
$ sort /usr/share/dict/words | head -n2 &
[1] 81089
$ A
A's
```

Press Enter, and the shell will print a "job done" message:

```
[1]+  Done                    sort /usr/share/dict/words | head -n2
$
```

Screen output from a background job can appear at any time while the job runs. To avoid this sort of messiness, redirect stdout to a file, then examine the file at your leisure:

```
$ sort /usr/share/dict/words | head -n2 > /tmp/results &
[1] 81089
$
[1]+  Done                    sort /usr/share/dict/words | head -n2 > /tmp/results
$ cat /tmp/results
A
A's
$
```

Other odd things happen when a background job attempts to read from stdin. The shell suspends the job, prints a *Stopped* message, and waits for input in the background. Demonstrate this by backgrounding cat with no arguments so it reads stdin:

```
$ cat &
[1] 82455
[1]+  Stopped                 cat
```

Jobs can't read input in the background, so bring the job into the foreground with fg and then supply the input:

```
$ fg
cat
Here is some input
```

```
Here is some input
⋮
```

After supplying all input, do any of the following:

- Continue running the command in the foreground until it completes.
- Suspend and background the command again by pressing Ctrl-Z followed by bg.
- End the input with Ctrl-D, or kill the command with Ctrl-C.

Backgrounding tips

Backgrounding is ideal for commands that take a long time to run, such as text editors during long editing sessions, or any program that opens its own windows. For example, programmers can save a lot of time by suspending their text editor rather than exiting. I've seen experienced engineers modify some code in their text editor, save and quit the editor, test the code, then relaunch the editor and hunt for the spot in the code where they'd left off. They lose 10–15 seconds to job-switching every time they quit the editor. If they instead suspend the editor (Ctrl-Z), test their code, and resume the editor (fg), they avoiding wasting time unnecessarily.

Backgrounding is also great for running a sequence of commands in the background using a conditional list. If any command within the list fails, the rest won't run and the job completes. (Just watch out for commands that read input, since they'll cause the job to suspend and wait for input.)

```
$ command1 && command2 && command3 &
```

Technique #10: Explicit Subshells

Each time you launch a simple command, it runs in a child process, as you saw in "Parent and Child Processes" on page 97. Command substitution and process substitution create subshells. There are times, however, when it's helpful to launch an extra subshell explicitly. To do so, simply enclose a command in parentheses and it runs in a subshell:

```
$ (cd /usr/local && ls)
bin   etc   games   lib   man   sbin   share
$ pwd
/home/smith                    "cd /usr/local" occurred in a subshell
```

When applied to a whole command, this technique isn't super useful, except maybe to save you from running a second cd command to return to your previous directory. However, if you place parentheses around one piece of a combined command, you can perform some useful tricks. A typical example is a pipeline that changes directory in the middle of execution. Suppose you have downloaded a compressed tar file, *package.tar.gz*, and you want to extract the files. A tar command to extract the files is:

```
$ tar xvf package.tar.gz
Makefile
src/
src/defs.h
src/main.c
⋮
```

The extraction occurs relative to the current directory.[8] What if you want to extract them into a different directory? You could cd to the other directory first and run tar (and then cd back), but you can also perform this task with a single command. The trick is to pipe the tarred data to a subshell that performs directory operations and runs tar as it reads from stdin:[9]

```
$ cat package.tar.gz | (mkdir -p /tmp/other && cd /tmp/other && tar xzvf -)
```

This technique also works to copy files from one directory *dir1* to another existing directory *dir2* using two tar processes, one writing to stdout and one reading from stdin:

```
$ tar czf - dir1 | (cd /tmp/dir2 && tar xvf -)
```

The same technique can copy files to an existing directory on another host via SSH:

```
$ tar czf - dir1 | ssh myhost '(cd /tmp/dir2 && tar xvf -)'
```

Which Techniques Create Subshells?

Many of the techniques in this chapter launch a subshell, which inherits the parent's environment (variables and their values) plus other shell context such as aliases. Other techniques only launch a child process. The simplest way to distinguish them is to evaluate the variable BASH_SUBSHELL, which will be nonzero for a subshell and zero otherwise. More details are in "Child Shells Versus Subshells" on page 102.

```
$ echo $BASH_SUBSHELL              Ordinary execution
0                                  Not a subshell
$ (echo $BASH_SUBSHELL)            Explicit subshell
1                                  Subshell
$ echo $(echo $BASH_SUBSHELL)      Command substitution
1                                  Subshell
$ cat <(echo $BASH_SUBSHELL)       Process substitution
1                                  Subshell
$ bash -c 'echo $BASH_SUBSHELL'    bash -c
0                                  Not a subshell
```

---

8 Assuming that the tar archive was built with relative paths—which is typical for downloaded software—not absolute paths.

9 This specific problem can be solved more simply with the tar option -C or --directory, which specifies a target directory. I'm just demonstrating the general technique of using a subshell.

It's tempting to view bash parentheses as if they simply group commands together, like parentheses in arithmetic. They do not. Each pair of parentheses causes a subshell to be launched.

Technique #11: Process Replacement

Normally when you run a command, the shell runs it in a separate process that is destroyed when the command exits, as described in "Parent and Child Processes" on page 97. You can change this behavior with the exec command, which is a shell builtin. It *replaces* the running shell (a process) with another command of your choice (another process). When the new command exits, no shell prompt will follow because the original shell is gone.

To demonstrate this, run a new shell manually and change its prompt:

```
$ bash              Run a child shell
$ PS1="Doomed> "    Change the new shell's prompt
Doomed> echo hello  Run any command you like
hello
```

Now exec a command and watch the new shell die:

```
Doomed> exec ls     ls replaces the child shell, runs, and exits
animals.txt
$                   A prompt from the original (parent) shell
```

Running exec May Be Fatal

If you run exec in a shell, the shell exits afterward. If the shell was running in a terminal window, the window closes. If the shell was a login shell, you will be logged out.

Why would you ever run exec? One reason is to conserve resources by not launching a second process. Shell scripts sometimes make use of this optimization by running exec on the final command in the script. If the script is run many times (say, millions or billions of executions), the savings might be worth it.

exec has a second ability—it can reassign stdin, stdout, and/or stderr for the current shell. This is most practical in a shell script, such as this toy example that prints information to a file, */tmp/outfile*:

```
#!/bin/bash
echo "My name is $USER"                                      > /tmp/outfile
echo "My current directory is $PWD"                         >> /tmp/outfile
echo "Guess how many lines are in the file /etc/hosts?" >> /tmp/outfile
wc -l /etc/hosts                                            >> /tmp/outfile
echo "Goodbye for now"                                      >> /tmp/outfile
```

Instead of redirecting the output of each command to */tmp/outfile* individually, use **exec** to redirect stdout to */tmp/outfile* for the entire script. Subsequent commands can simply print to stdout:

```
#!/bin/bash
# Redirect stdout for this script
exec > /tmp/outfile2
# All subsequent commands print to /tmp/outfile2
echo "My name is $USER"
echo "My current directory is $PWD"
echo "Guess how many lines are in the file /etc/hosts?"
wc -l /etc/hosts
echo "Goodbye for now"
```

Run this script and examine the file */tmp/outfile2* to see the results:

```
$ cat /tmp/outfile2
My name is smith
My current directory is /home/smith
Guess how many lines are in the file /etc/hosts?
122 /etc/hosts
Goodbye for now
```

You probably won't use **exec** often, but it's there when you need it.

Summary

Now you have 13 techniques for running a command—the 11 in this chapter plus simple commands and pipelines. Table 7-2 reviews some common use cases for different techniques.

Table 7-2. Common idioms for running commands

Problem	Solution
Sending stdout from one program to stdin of another	Pipelines
Inserting output (stdout) into a command	Command substitution
Providing output (stdout) to a command that doesn't read from stdin, but does read disk files	Process substitution
Executing one string as a command	`bash -c`, or piping to `bash`
Printing multiple commands on stdout and executing them	Piping to `bash`
Executing many similar commands in a row	`xargs`, or constructing the commands as strings and piping them to `bash`

Problem	Solution
Managing commands that depend on one other's success	Conditional lists
Running several commands at a time	Backgrounding
Running several commands at a time that depend on one another's success	Backgrounding a conditional list
Running one command on a remote host	Run `ssh` *`host command`*
Changing directory in the middle of a pipeline	Explicit subshells
Running a command later	Unconditional list with `sleep` followed by the command
Redirecting to/from protected files	Run `sudo bash -c` *`"command > file"`*

The next two chapters will teach you to combine techniques to achieve business goals efficiently.

## CHAPTER 8

Building a Brash One-Liner

Remember this long, intricate command from the preface?

```
$ paste <(echo {1..10}.jpg | sed 's/ /\n/g') \
        <(echo {0..9}.jpg | sed 's/ /\n/g') \
  | sed 's/^/mv /' \
  | bash
```

Such magical incantations are called *brash one-liners*.[1] Let's take this one apart to understand what it does and how it works. The innermost echo commands use brace expansion to generate lists of JPEG filenames:

```
$ echo {1..10}.jpg
1.jpg 2.jpg 3.jpg ... 10.jpg
$ echo {0..9}.jpg
0.jpg 1.jpg 2.jpg ... 9.jpg
```

Piping the filenames to sed replaces space characters with newlines:

```
$ echo {1..10}.jpg | sed 's/ /\n/g'
1.jpg
2.jpg
⋮
10.jpg
$ echo {0..9}.jpg | sed 's/ /\n/g'
0.jpg
1.jpg
⋮
9.jpg
```

---

[1] The earliest use of this term (that I know of) is the manpage for lorder(1) (*https://oreil.ly/ro621*) in BSD Unix 4.x. Thanks to Bob Byrnes for finding it.

The `paste` command prints the two lists side by side. Process substitution allows `paste` to read the two lists as if they were files:

```
$ paste <(echo {1..10}.jpg | sed 's/ /\n/g') \
        <(echo {0..9}.jpg | sed 's/ /\n/g')
1.jpg   0.jpg
2.jpg   1.jpg
⋮
10.jpg  9.jpg
```

Prepending `mv` to each line prints a sequence of strings that are `mv` commands:

```
$ paste <(echo {1..10}.jpg | sed 's/ /\n/g') \
        <(echo {0..9}.jpg | sed 's/ /\n/g') \
  | sed 's/^/mv /'
mv 1.jpg   0.jpg
mv 2.jpg   1.jpg
⋮
mv 10.jpg  9.jpg
```

The purpose of the command is now revealed: it generates 10 commands to rename the image files *1.jpg* through *10.jpg*. The new names are *0.jpg* through *9.jpg*, respectively. Piping the output to `bash` executes the `mv` commands:

```
$ paste <(echo {1..10}.jpg | sed 's/ /\n/g') \
        <(echo {0..9}.jpg | sed 's/ /\n/g') \
  | sed 's/^/mv /' \
  | bash
```

Brash one-liners are like puzzles. You're faced with a business problem, such as renaming a set of files, and you apply your toolbox to construct a Linux command to solve it. Brash one-liners challenge your creativity and build your skills.

In this chapter, you'll create brash one-liners like the preceding one, step-by-step, using the following magical formula:

1. Invent a command that solves a piece of the puzzle.

2. Run the command and check the output.

3. Recall the command from history and tweak it.

4. Repeat steps 2 and 3 until the command produces the desired result.

This chapter will give your brain a workout. Expect to feel puzzled at times by the examples. Just take things one step at a time, and run the commands on a computer as you read them.

Some brash one-liners in this chapter are too wide for a single line, so I've split them onto multiple lines using backslashes. We do not, however, call them brash two-liners (or brash seven-liners).

Get Ready to Be Brash

Before you launch into creating brash one-liners, take a moment to get into the right mindset:

- Be flexible.
- Think about where to start.
- Know your testing tools.

I'll discuss each of these ideas in turn.

Be Flexible

A key to writing brash one-liners is *flexibility*. You've learned some awesome tools by this point—a core set of Linux programs (and umpteen ways to run them) along with command history, command-line editing, and more. You can combine these tools in many ways, and a given problem usually has multiple solutions.

Even the simplest Linux tasks can be accomplished in many ways. Consider how you might list *.jpg* files in your current directory. I'll bet 99.9% of Linux users would run a command like this:

```
$ ls *.jpg
```

But this is just one solution of many. For example, you could list *all* the files in the directory and then use grep to match only the names ending in *.jpg*:

```
$ ls | grep '\.jpg$'
```

Why would you choose this solution? Well, you saw an example in "Long Argument Lists" on page 123, when a directory contained so many files that they couldn't be listed by pattern matching. The technique of *grepping for a filename extension* is a robust, general approach for solving all sorts of problems. What's important here is to be flexible and understand your tools so you can apply the best one in your time of need. That is a wizard's skill when creating brash one-liners.

All of the following commands list *.jpg* files in the current directory. Try to figure out how each command works:

```
$ echo $(ls *.jpg)
$ bash -c 'ls *.jpg'
$ cat <(ls *.jpg)
$ find . -maxdepth 1 -type f -name \*.jpg -print
$ ls > tmp && grep '\.jpg$' tmp && rm -f tmp
$ paste <(echo ls) <(echo \*.jpg) | bash
$ bash -c 'exec $(paste <(echo ls) <(echo \*.jpg))'
$ echo 'monkey *.jpg' | sed 's/monkey/ls/' | bash
$ python -c 'import os; os.system("ls *.jpg")'
```

Are the results identical or do some commands behave a bit differently? Can you come up with any other suitable commands?

Think About Where to Start

Every brash one-liner begins with the output of a simple command. That output might be the contents of a file, part of a file, a directory listing, a sequence of numbers or letters, a list of users, a date and time, or other data. Your first challenge, therefore, is to produce the initial data for your command.

For example, if you want to know the 17th letter of the English alphabet, then your initial data could be 26 letters produced by brace expansion:

```
$ echo {A..Z}
A B C D E F G H I J K L M N O P Q R S T U V W X Y Z
```

Once you can produce this output, the next step is deciding how to massage it to fit your goal. Do you need to slice the output by rows or columns? Join the output with other information? Transform the output in a more complicated way? Look to the programs in Chapters 1 and 5 to do that work, like grep and sed and cut, and apply them using the techniques of Chapter 7.

For this example, you could print the 17th field with awk, or remove spaces with sed and locate the 17th character with cut:

```
$ echo {A..Z} | awk '{print $(17)}'
Q
$ echo {A..Z} | sed 's/ //g' | cut -c17
Q
```

As another example, if you want to print the months of the year, your initial data could be the numbers 1 through 12, again produced by brace expansion:

```
$ echo {1..12}
1 2 3 4 5 6 7 8 9 10 11 12
```

From there, augment the brace expansion so it forms dates for the first day of each month (from 2021-01-01 through 2021-12-01); then run date -d on each line to produce month names:

```
$ echo 2021-{01..12}-01 | xargs -n1 date +%B -d
January
February
March
⋮
December
```

Or, suppose you want to know the length of the longest filename in the current directory. Your initial data could be a directory listing:

```
$ ls
animals.txt  cartoon-mascots.txt  ...  zebra-stripes.txt
```

From there, use awk to generate commands to count characters in each filename with wc -c:

```
$ ls | awk '{print "echo -n", $0, "| wc -c"}'
echo -n "animals.txt" | wc -c
echo -n "cartoon-mascots.txt | wc -c"
⋮
echo -n "zebra-stripes.txt | wc -c"
```

(The -n option prevents echo from printing newline characters, which would throw off each count by one.) Finally, pipe the commands to bash to run them, sort the numeric results from high to low, and grab the maximum value (the first line) with head -n1:

```
$ ls | awk '{print "echo -n", $0, "| wc -c"}' | bash | sort -nr | head -n1
23
```

This last example was tricky, generating pipelines as strings and passing them to a further pipeline. Nevertheless, the general principle is the same: figure out your starting data and manipulate it to fit your needs.

Know Your Testing Tools

Building a brash one-liner may require trial and error. The following tools and techniques will help you try different solutions quickly:

Use command history and command-line editing.
> Don't retype commands while you experiment. Use techniques from Chapter 3 to recall previous commands, tweak them, and run them.

Add echo to test your expressions.
> If you aren't sure how an expression will evaluate, print it with echo beforehand to see the evaluated results on stdout.

Use `ls` *or add* `echo` *to test destructive commands.*

If your command invokes `rm`, `mv`, `cp`, or other commands that might overwrite or remove files, place `echo` in front of them to confirm which files will be affected. (So, instead of executing `rm`, execute `echo` `rm`.) Another safety tactic is to replace `rm` with `ls` to list files that would be removed.

Insert a `tee` *to view intermediate results.*

If you want to view the output (stdout) in the middle of a long pipeline, insert the `tee` command to save output to a file for examination. The following command saves the output from `command3` in the file *outfile*, while piping that same output to `command4`:

```
$ command1 | command2 | command3 | tee outfile | command4 | command5
$ less outfile
```

OK, let's build some brash one-liners!

Inserting a Filename into a Sequence

This brash one-liner is similar to the one that opened the chapter (renaming *.jpg* files), but more detailed. It's also a real situation I faced while writing this book. Like the previous one-liner, it combines two techniques from Chapter 7: process substitution and piping to `bash`. The result is a repeatable pattern for solving similar problems.

I wrote this book on a Linux computer using a typesetting language called AsciiDoc (*https://asciidoc.org*). The language details aren't important here; what matters is each chapter was a separate file, and originally there were 10 of them:

```
$ ls
ch01.asciidoc  ch03.asciidoc  ch05.asciidoc  ch07.asciidoc  ch09.asciidoc
ch02.asciidoc  ch04.asciidoc  ch06.asciidoc  ch08.asciidoc  ch10.asciidoc
```

At some point, I decided to insert an 11th chapter between Chapters 2 and 3. That meant renaming some files. Chapters 3–10 had to become 4–11, leaving a gap so I could make a new Chapter 3 (*ch03.asciidoc*). I could have renamed the files manually, starting with *ch11.asciidoc* and working backward:[2]

```
$ mv ch10.asciidoc ch11.asciidoc
$ mv ch09.asciidoc ch10.asciidoc
$ mv ch08.asciidoc ch09.asciidoc
⋮
$ mv ch03.asciidoc ch04.asciidoc
```

---

2 Starting with *ch03.asciidoc* and working forward would be dangerous—can you see why? If not, create these files with the command `touch ch{01..10}.asciidoc` and try it yourself.

But this method is tedious (imagine if there were 1,000 files instead of 11!), so instead, I generated the necessary mv commands and piped them to bash. Take a good look at the preceding mv commands and think for a moment how you might create them.

Focus first on the original filenames *ch03.asciidoc* through *ch10.asciidoc*. You could print them using brace expansion such as ch{10..03}.asciidoc, like the first example in this chapter, but to practice a little flexibility, use the seq -w command to print the numbers:

```
$ seq -w 10 -1 3
10
09
08
⋮
03
```

Then turn this numeric sequence into filenames by piping it to sed:

```
$ seq -w 10 -1 3 | sed 's/\(.*\)/ch\1.asciidoc/'
ch10.asciidoc
ch09.asciidoc
⋮
ch03.asciidoc
```

You now have a list of the original filenames. Do likewise for Chapters 4–11 to create the destination filenames:

```
$ seq -w 11 -1 4 | sed 's/\(.*\)/ch\1.asciidoc/'
ch11.asciidoc
ch10.asciidoc
⋮
ch04.asciidoc
```

To form the mv commands, you need to print the original and new filenames side by side. The first example in this chapter solved the "side by side" problem with paste, and it used process substitution to treat the two printed lists as files. Do the same here:

```
$ paste <(seq -w 10 -1 3 | sed 's/\(.*\)/ch\1.asciidoc/') \
        <(seq -w 11 -1 4 | sed 's/\(.*\)/ch\1.asciidoc/')
ch10.asciidoc   ch11.asciidoc
ch09.asciidoc   ch10.asciidoc
⋮
ch03.asciidoc   ch04.asciidoc
```

The preceding command might look like a lot of typing, but with command history and Emacs-style command-line editing, it's really not. To go from the single "seq and sed" line to the `paste` command:

1. Recall the previous command from history with the up arrow.

2. Press Ctrl-A and then Ctrl-K to cut the whole line.

3. Type the word `paste` followed by a space.

4. Press Ctrl-Y twice to create two copies of the `seq` and `sed` commands.

5. Use movement and editing keystrokes to modify the second copy.

6. And so on.

Prepend `mv` to each line by piping the output to `sed`, printing exactly the `mv` commands you need:

```
$ paste <(seq -w 10 -1 3 | sed 's/\(.*\)/ch\1.asciidoc/') \
        <(seq -w 11 -1 4 | sed 's/\(.*\)/ch\1.asciidoc/') \
  | sed 's/^/mv /'
mv ch10.asciidoc    ch11.asciidoc
mv ch09.asciidoc    ch10.asciidoc
⋮
mv ch03.asciidoc    ch04.asciidoc
```

As the final step, pipe the commands to `bash` for execution:

```
$ paste <(seq -w 10 -1 3 | sed 's/\(.*\)/ch\1.asciidoc/') \
        <(seq -w 11 -1 4 | sed 's/\(.*\)/ch\1.asciidoc/') \
  | sed 's/^/mv /' \
  | bash
```

I used exactly this solution for my book. After the `mv` commands ran, the resulting files were Chapters 1, 2, and 4–11, leaving a gap for a new Chapter 3:

```
$ ls ch*.asciidoc
ch01.asciidoc  ch04.asciidoc  ch06.asciidoc  ch08.asciidoc  ch10.asciidoc
ch02.asciidoc  ch05.asciidoc  ch07.asciidoc  ch09.asciidoc  ch11.asciidoc
```

The pattern I just presented is reusable in all kinds of situations to run a sequence of related commands:

1. Generate the command arguments as lists on stdout.

2. Print the lists side by side with `paste` and process substitution.

3. Prepend a command name with `sed` by replacing the beginning-of-line character (^) with a program name and a space.

4. Pipe the results to `bash`.

Checking Matched Pairs of Files

This brash-one liner is inspired by a real use of Mediawiki, the software that powers Wikipedia and thousands of other wikis. Mediawiki allows users to upload images for display. Most users follow a manual process via web forms: click Choose File to bring up a file dialog, navigate to an image file and select it, add a descriptive comment in the form, and click Upload. Wiki administrators use a more automated method: a script that reads a whole directory and uploads its images. Each image file (say, *bald_eagle.jpg*) is paired with a text file (*bald_eagle.txt*) containing a descriptive comment about the image.

Imagine that you're faced with a huge directory containing only JPEG and TXT files. You want to confirm that every image file has a matching text file and vice versa. Here's a smaller version of that directory:

```
$ ls
bald_eagle.jpg  blue_jay.jpg  cardinal.txt  robin.jpg  wren.jpg
bald_eagle.txt  cardinal.jpg  oriole.txt    robin.txt  wren.txt
```

Let's develop two different solutions to identify any unmatched files. For the first solution, create two lists, one for the JPEG files and one for the text files, and use `cut` to strip off their file extensions *.txt* and *.jpg*:

```
$ ls *.jpg | cut -d. -f1
bald_eagle
blue_jay
cardinal
robin
wren
$ ls *.txt | cut -d. -f1
bald_eagle
cardinal
oriole
robin
wren
```

Then compare the lists with `diff` using process substitution:

```
$ diff <(ls *.jpg | cut -d. -f1) <(ls *.txt | cut -d. -f1)
2d1
< blue_jay
3a3
> oriole
```

You could stop here, because the output indicates that the first list has an extra *blue_jay* (implying *blue_jay.jpg*) and the second list has an extra *oriole* (implying *oriole.txt*). Nevertheless, let's make the results more precise. Eliminate unwanted lines by grepping for the characters < and > at the beginning of each line:

```
$ diff <(ls *.jpg | cut -d. -f1) <(ls *.txt | cut -d. -f1) \
  | grep '^[<>]'
< blue_jay
> oriole
```

Then use awk to append the correct file extension to each filename ($2), based on whether the filename is preceded by a leading < or >:

```
$ diff <(ls *.jpg | cut -d. -f1) <(ls *.txt | cut -d. -f1) \
  | grep '^[<>]' \
  | awk '/^</{print $2 ".jpg"} /^>/{print $2 ".txt"}'
blue_jay.jpg
oriole.txt
```

You now have your list of unmatched files. However, this solution has a subtle bug. Suppose the current directory contained the filename *yellow.canary.jpg*, which has two dots. The preceding command would produce incorrect output:

```
blue_jay.jpg
oriole.txt
yellow.jpg                      This is wrong
```

This problem occurs because the two cut commands remove characters from the first dot onward, instead of the last dot onward, so *yellow.canary.jpg* is truncated to *yellow* rather than *yellow.canary*. To fix this issue, replace cut with sed to remove characters from the last dot to the end of the string:

```
$ diff <(ls *.jpg | sed 's/\.[^.]*$//') \
       <(ls *.txt | sed 's/\.[^.]*$//') \
  | grep '^[<>]' \
  | awk '/</{print $2 ".jpg"} />/{print $2 ".txt"}'
blue_jay.txt
oriole.jpg
yellow.canary.txt
```

The first solution is now complete. The second solution takes a different approach. Instead of applying diff to two lists, generate a single list and weed out matched pairs of filenames. Begin by removing the file extensions with sed (using the same sed script as before) and count the occurrences of each string with uniq -c:

```
$ ls *.{jpg,txt} \
  | sed 's/\.[^.]*$//' \
  | uniq -c
      2 bald_eagle
      1 blue_jay
      2 cardinal
      1 oriole
```

```
2 robin
2 wren
1 yellow.canary
```

Each line of output contains either the number 2, representing a matched pair of filenames, or 1, representing an unmatched filename. Use `awk` to isolate lines that begin with whitespace and a 1, and print only the second field:

```
$ ls *.{jpg,txt} \
  | sed 's/\.[^.]*$//' \
  | uniq -c \
  | awk '/^ *1 /{print $2}'
blue_jay
oriole
yellow.canary
```

For the final step, how can you add the missing file extensions? Don't bother with any complicated string manipulations. Just use `ls` to list the actual files in the current directory. Stick a dot and an asterisk onto the end of each line of output with `awk`:

```
$ ls *.{jpg,txt} \
  | sed 's/\.[^.]*$//' \
  | uniq -c \
  | awk '/^ *1 /{print $2 ".*"}'
blue_jay.*
oriole.*
yellow.canary.*
```

and feed the lines to `ls` via command substitution. The shell performs pattern matching, and `ls` prints the full filenames with extensions. Done!

```
$ ls -1 $(ls *.{jpg,txt} \
  | sed 's/\.[^.]*$//' \
  | uniq -c \
  | awk '/^ *1 /{print $2 ".*"}')
blue_jay.jpg
oriole.txt
yellow.canary.jpg
```

Generating a CDPATH from Your Home Directory

In the section "Organize Your Home Directory for Fast Navigation" on page 55, you wrote a complicated CDPATH line by hand. It began with $HOME, followed by all subdirectories of $HOME, and ended with the relative path `..` (parent directory):

```
CDPATH=$HOME:$HOME/Work:$HOME/Family:$HOME/Finances:$HOME/Linux:$HOME/Music:..
```

Let's create a brash one-liner to generate that CDPATH line automatically, suitable for insertion into a bash configuration file. Begin with the list of subdirectories in $HOME, using a subshell to prevent the cd command from changing your shell's current directory:

```
$ (cd && ls -d */)
Family/  Finances/  Linux/  Music/  Work/
```

Add $HOME/ in front of each directory with sed:

```
$ (cd && ls -d */) | sed 's/^/$HOME\//g'
$HOME/Family/
$HOME/Finances/
$HOME/Linux/
$HOME/Music/
$HOME/Work/
```

The preceding sed script is slightly complicated because the replacement string, $HOME/, contains a forward slash, and sed substitutions also use the forward slash as a separator. That's why my slash is escaped: $HOME\/. To simplify things, recall from "Substitution and Slashes" on page 91 that sed accepts any convenient character as a separator. Let's use at signs (@) instead of forward slashes so no escaping is needed:

```
$ (cd && ls -d */) | sed 's@^@$HOME/@g'
$HOME/Family/
$HOME/Finances/
$HOME/Linux/
$HOME/Music/
$HOME/Work/
```

Next, lop off the final forward slash with another sed expression:

```
$ (cd && ls -d */) | sed -e 's@^@$HOME/@' -e 's@/$@@'
$HOME/Family
$HOME/Finances
$HOME/Linux
$HOME/Music
$HOME/Work
```

Print the output on a single line using echo and command substitution. Notice that you no longer need plain parentheses around cd and ls to create a subshell explicitly, because command substitution creates a subshell of its own:

```
$ echo $(cd && ls -d */ | sed -e 's@^@$HOME/@' -e 's@/$@@')
$HOME/Family $HOME/Finances $HOME/Linux $HOME/Music $HOME/Work
```

Add the first directory $HOME and the final relative directory ..:

```
$ echo '$HOME' \
       $(cd && ls -d */ | sed -e 's@^@$HOME/@' -e 's@/$@@') \
       ..
$HOME $HOME/Family $HOME/Finances $HOME/Linux $HOME/Music $HOME/Work ..
```

Change spaces to colons by piping all the output so far to `tr`:

```
$ echo '$HOME' \
    $(cd && ls -d */ | sed -e 's@^@$HOME/@' -e 's@/$@@') \
    .. \
  | tr ' ' ':'
$HOME:$HOME/Family:$HOME/Finances:$HOME/Linux:$HOME/Music:$HOME/Work:..
```

Finally, add the `CDPATH` environment variable, and you have generated a variable definition to paste into a `bash` configuration file. Store this command in a script to generate the line anytime, like when you add a new subdirectory to `$HOME`:

```
$ echo 'CDPATH=$HOME' \
    $(cd && ls -d */ | sed -e 's@^@$HOME/@' -e 's@/$@@') \
    .. \
  | tr ' ' ':'
CDPATH=$HOME:$HOME/Family:$HOME/Finances:$HOME/Linux:$HOME/Music:$HOME/Work:..
```

Generating Test Files

A common task in the software industry is testing—feeding a wide variety of data to a program to validate that the program behaves as intended. The next brash one-liner generates one thousand files containing random text that could be used in software testing. The number one thousand is arbitrary; you can generate as many files as you want.

The solution will select words randomly from a large text file and create one thousand smaller files with random contents and lengths. A perfect source file is the system dictionary */usr/share/dict/words*, which contains 102,305 words, each on its own line.

```
$ wc -l /usr/share/dict/words
102305 /usr/share/dict/words
```

To produce this brash one-liner, you'll need to solve four puzzles:

1. Randomly shuffling the dictionary file
2. Selecting a random number of lines from the dictionary file
3. Creating an output file to hold the results
4. Running your solution one thousand times

To shuffle the dictionary into random order, use the aptly named command `shuf`. Each run of the command `shuf /usr/share/dict/words` produces more than a hundred thousand lines of output, so peek at the first few random lines using `head`:

```
$ shuf /usr/share/dict/words | head -n3
evermore
shirttail
tertiary
$ shuf /usr/share/dict/words | head -n3
interactively
opt
perjurer
```

Your first puzzle is solved. Next, how can you select a random quantity of lines from the shuffled dictionary? shuf has an option, -n, to print a given number of lines, but you want the value to change for each output file you create. Fortunately, bash has a variable, RANDOM, that holds a random positive integer between 0 and 32,767. Its value changes every time you access the variable:

```
$ echo $RANDOM $RANDOM $RANDOM
7855 11134 262
```

Therefore, run shuf with the option -n $RANDOM to print a random number of random lines. Again, the full output could be very long, so pipe the results to wc -l to confirm that the number of lines changes with each execution:

```
$ shuf -n $RANDOM /usr/share/dict/words | wc -l
9922
$ shuf -n $RANDOM /usr/share/dict/words | wc -l
32465
```

You've solved the second puzzle. Next, you need one thousand output files, or more specifically, one thousand different filenames. To generate filenames, run the program pwgen, which generates random strings of letters and digits:

```
$ pwgen
eng9nooG ier6YeVu AhZ7naeG Ap3quail poo2Ooj9 OYiuri9m iQush0E voo3Eph1
IeQu7mi6 eipaC2ti exah8iNg oeGhahm8 airooJ8N eiZ7neez Dah8Vooj dixiV1fu
Xiejoti6 ieshei2K iX4isohk Ohm5gaol Ri9ah4eX Aiv1ahg3 Shaew3ko zohB4geu
⋮
```

Add the option -N1 to generate just a single string, and specify the string length (10) as an argument:

```
$ pwgen -N1 10
ieb2ESheiw
```

Optionally, make the string look more like the name of a text file, using command substitution:

```
$ echo $(pwgen -N1 10).txt
ohTie8aifo.txt
```

Third puzzle complete! You now have all the tools to generate a single random text file. Use the -o option of shuf to save its output in a file:

```
$ mkdir -p /tmp/randomfiles && cd /tmp/randomfiles
$ shuf -n $RANDOM -o $(pwgen -N1 10).txt /usr/share/dict/words
```

and check the results:

```
$ ls                            List the new file
Ahxiedie2f.txt
$ wc -l Ahxiedie2f.txt          How many lines does it contain?
13544 Ahxiedie2f.txt
$ head -n3 Ahxiedie2f.txt       Peek at the first few lines
saviors
guerillas
forecaster
```

Looks good! The final puzzle is how to run the preceding shuf command one thousand times. You could certainly use a loop:

```
for i in {1..1000}; do
  shuf -n $RANDOM -o $(pwgen -N1 10).txt /usr/share/dict/words
done
```

but that's not as fun as creating a brash one-liner. Instead, let's pregenerate the commands, as strings, and pipe them to bash. As a test, print your desired command once using echo. Add single quotes to ensure that $RANDOM doesn't evaluate and pwgen doesn't run:

```
$ echo 'shuf -n $RANDOM -o $(pwgen -N1 10).txt /usr/share/dict/words'
shuf -n $RANDOM -o $(pwgen -N1 10).txt /usr/share/dict/words
```

This command can easily be piped to bash for execution:

```
$ echo 'shuf -n $RANDOM -o $(pwgen -N1 10).txt /usr/share/dict/words' | bash
$ ls
eiFohpies1.txt
```

Now, print the command one thousand times using the yes command piped to head, then pipe the results to bash, and you've solved the fourth puzzle:

```
$ yes 'shuf -n $RANDOM -o $(pwgen -N1 10).txt /usr/share/dict/words' \
  | head -n 1000 \
  | bash
$ ls
Aen1lee0ir.txt   IeKaveixa6.txt   ahDee9lah2.txt   paeR1Poh3d.txt
Ahxiedie2f.txt   Kas8ooJahK.txt   aoc0Yoohoh.txt   sohl7Nohho.txt
CudieNgee4.txt   Oe5ophae8e.txt   haiV9mahNg.txt   uchiek3Eew.txt
⋮
```

If you'd prefer one thousand random image files instead of text files, use the same technique (yes, head, and bash) and replace shuf with a command that generates a random image. Here's a brash one-liner that I adapted from a solution by Mark Setchell on Stack Overflow (*https://oreil.ly/ruDwG*). It runs the command convert, from the graphics package ImageMagick, to produce random images of size 100 x 100 pixels consisting of multicolored squares:

```
$ yes 'convert -size 8x8 xc: +noise Random -scale 100x100 $(pwgen -N1 10).png' \
  | head -n 1000 \
  | bash
$ ls
Bahdo4Yaop.png   Um8ju8gie5.png   aing1QuaiX.png   ohi4ziNuwo.png
Eem5leijae.png   Va7ohchiep.png   eiMoog1kou.png   ohnohwu4Ei.png
Eozaing1ie.png   Zaev4Quien.png   hiecima2Ye.png   quaepaiY9t.png
⋮
$ display Bahdo4Yaop.png          View the first image
```

Generating Empty Files

Sometimes all you need for testing is lots of files with different names, even if they're empty. Generating a thousand empty files named *file0001.txt* through *file1000.txt* is as simple as:

```
$ mkdir /tmp/empties          Create a directory for the files
$ cd /tmp/empties
$ touch file{01..1000}.txt     Generate the files
```

If you prefer more interesting filenames, grab them randomly from the system dictionary. Use grep to limit the names to lowercase letters for simplicity (avoiding spaces, apostrophes, and other characters that would be special to the shell):

```
$ grep '^[a-z]*$' /usr/share/dict/words
a
aardvark
aardvarks
⋮
```

Shuffle the names with shuf and print the first thousand with head:

```
$ grep '^[a-z]*$' /usr/share/dict/words | shuf | head -n1000
triplicating
quadruplicates
podiatrists
⋮
```

Finally, pipe the results to xargs to create the files with touch:

```
$ grep '^[a-z]*$' /usr/share/dict/words | shuf | head -n1000 | xargs touch
$ ls
abases         distinctly      magnolia        sadden
abets          distrusts       maintaining     sales
aboard         divided         malformation    salmon
⋮
```

Summary

I hope the examples in this chapter helped to build your skills in writing brash one-liners. Several of them provided reusable patterns that you may find useful in other situations.

One caveat: brash one-liners are not the only solution in town. They're just one approach to working efficiently at the command line. Sometimes you'll get more bang for the buck by writing a shell script. Other times you'll find better solutions with a programming language such as Perl or Python. Nevertheless, brash one-liner-writing is a vital skill for performing critical tasks with speed and style.

Leveraging Text Files

Plain text is the most common data format on many Linux systems. The content sent from command to command in most pipelines is text. Programmers' source code files, system configuration files in */etc*, and HTML and Markdown files are all text files. Email messages are text; even attachments are stored as text internally for transport. You might even store everyday files like shopping lists and personal notes as text.

Contrast this with today's internet, which is a mishmash of streaming audio and video, social media posts, in-browser documents in Google Docs and Office 365, PDFs, and other rich media. (Not to mention the data handled by mobile apps, which have hidden the concept of a "file" from a whole generation.) Against this backdrop, plain-text files seem almost quaint.

Nevertheless, any text file can become a rich source of data that you can mine with carefully crafted Linux commands, especially if the text is structured. Each line in the file */etc/passwd*, for example, represents a Linux user and has seven fields, including username, numeric user ID, home directory, and more. The fields are separated by colons, making the file easily parsed by `cut -d:` or `awk -F:`. Here's a command that prints all usernames (the first field) alphabetically:

```
$ cut -d: -f1 /etc/passwd | sort
avahi
backup
daemon
⋮
```

And here's one that separates human users from system accounts by their numeric user IDs and sends users a welcome email. Let's build this brash one-liner step-by-step. First, use awk to print the usernames (field 1) when the numeric user ID (field 3) is 1000 or greater:

```
$ awk -F: '$3>=1000 {print $1}' /etc/passwd
jones
smith
```

Then produce greetings by piping to xargs:

```
$ awk -F: '$3>=1000 {print $1}' /etc/passwd \
  | xargs -I@ echo "Hi there, @!"
Hi there, jones!
Hi there, smith!
```

Then generate commands (strings) to pipe each greeting to the mail command, which sends email to a given user with a given subject line (-s):

```
$ awk -F: '$3>=1000 {print $1}' /etc/passwd \
  | xargs -I@ echo 'echo "Hi there, @!" | mail -s greetings @'
echo "Hi there, jones!" | mail -s greetings jones
echo "Hi there, smith!" | mail -s greetings smith
```

Finally, pipe the generated commands to bash to send the emails (no output will appear on the screen):

```
$ awk -F: '$3>=1000 {print $1}' /etc/passwd \
  | xargs -I@ echo 'echo "Hi there, @!" | mail -s greetings @' \
  | bash
```

The preceding solutions, like many others in this book, begin with an existing text file and manipulate its contents with commands. It's time to reverse that approach and intentionally *design new text files* that partner well with Linux commands.[1] This is a winning strategy to get work done efficiently on a Linux system. All it takes is four steps:

1. Notice a business problem you want to solve that involves data.

2. Store the data in a text file in a convenient format.

3. Invent Linux commands that process the file to solve the problem.

4. (*Optional.*) Capture those commands in scripts, aliases, or functions to be simpler to run.

In this chapter, you'll construct a variety of structured text files, and create commands to process them, to solve several business problems.

---

[1] This approach is similar to designing a database schema to work well with known queries.

A First Example: Finding Files

Suppose your home directory contains tens of thousands of files and subdirectories, and every so often, you can't remember where you put one of them. The find command locates a file by name, such as *animals.txt*:

```
$ find $HOME -name animals.txt -print
/home/smith/Work/Writing/Books/Lists/animals.txt
```

but find is slow because it searches your entire home directory, and you need to locate files regularly. This is step 1, noticing a business problem that involves data: finding files in your home directory quickly by name.

Step 2 is storing the data in a text file in a convenient format. Run find once to build a list of all your files and directories, one file path per line, and store it in a hidden file:

```
$ find $HOME -print > $HOME/.ALLFILES
$ head -n3 $HOME/.ALLFILES
/home/smith
/home/smith/Work
/home/smith/Work/resume.pdf
⋮
```

Now you have the data: a line-by-line index of your files. Step 3 is inventing Linux commands to speed up searches for files, and for that, use grep. It's much quicker to grep through a large file than to run find in a large directory tree:

```
$ grep animals.txt $HOME/.ALLFILES
/home/smith/Work/Writing/Books/Lists/animals.txt
```

Step 4 is to make the command easier to run. Write a one-line script named ff, for "find files," that runs grep with any user-supplied options and a search string, as in Example 9-1.

Example 9-1. The ff script

```
#!/bin/bash
# $@ means all arguments provided to the script
grep "$@" $HOME/.ALLFILES
```

Make the script executable and place it into any directory in your search path, such as your personal *bin* subdirectory:

```
$ chmod +x ff
$ echo $PATH                                    Check your search path
/home/smith/bin:/usr/local/bin:/usr/bin:/bin
$ mv ff ~/bin
```

Run ff anytime to locate files quickly when you can't remember where you put them.

```
$ ff animal
/home/smith/Work/Writing/Books/Lists/animals.txt
$ ff -i animal | less                          Case-insensitive grep
/home/smith/Work/Writing/Books/Lists/animals.txt
/home/smith/Vacations/Zoos/Animals/pandas.txt
/home/smith/Vacations/Zoos/Animals/tigers.txt
⋮
$ ff -i animal | wc -l                          How many matches?
16
```

Rerun the find command every so often to update the index. (Or better yet, create a scheduled job with cron; see "Learn cron, crontab, and at" on page 193.) Voilà—you've built a fast, flexible file-search utility out of two small commands. Linux systems provide other applications that index and search files quickly, such as the locate command and the search utilities in GNOME, KDE Plasma, and other desktop environments, but that's beside the point. Look how easy it was to build it *yourself*. And the key to success was to create a text file in a simple format.

Checking Domain Expiration

For the next example, suppose you own some internet domain names and want to keep track of when they expire so you can renew them. That's step 1, identify the business problem. Step 2 is to create a file of those domain names, such as *domains.txt*, one domain name per line:

```
example.com
oreilly.com
efficientlinux.com
⋮
```

Step 3 is to invent commands that leverage this text file to determine expiration dates. Start with the whois command, which queries a domain registrar for information about a domain:

```
$ whois example.com | less
Domain Name: EXAMPLE.COM
Registry Domain ID: 2336799_DOMAIN_COM-VRSN
Registrar WHOIS Server: whois.iana.org
Updated Date: 2021-08-14T07:01:44Z
Creation Date: 1995-08-14T04:00:00Z
Registry Expiry Date: 2022-08-13T04:00:00Z
⋮
```

The expiration date is preceded by the string "Registry Expiry Date", which you can isolate with grep and awk:

```
$ whois example.com | grep 'Registry Expiry Date:'
Registry Expiry Date: 2022-08-13T04:00:00Z
$ whois example.com | grep 'Registry Expiry Date:' | awk '{print $4}'
2022-08-13T04:00:00Z
```

Make the date more readable via the `date --date` command, which can convert a date string from one format to another:

```
$ date --date 2022-08-13T04:00:00Z
Sat Aug 13 00:00:00 EDT 2022
$ date --date 2022-08-13T04:00:00Z +'%Y-%m-%d'          Year-month-day format
2022-08-13
```

Use command substitution to feed the date string from `whois` to the `date` command:

```
$ echo $(whois example.com | grep 'Registry Expiry Date:' | awk '{print $4}')
2022-08-13T04:00:00Z
$ date \
  --date $(whois example.com \
           | grep 'Registry Expiry Date:' \
           | awk '{print $4}') \
  +'%Y-%m-%d'
2022-08-13
```

You now have a command that queries a registrar and prints an expiration date. Create a script `check-expiry`, shown in Example 9-2, that runs the preceding command and prints the expiration date, a tab, and the domain name:

```
$ ./check-expiry example.com
2022-08-13       example.com
```

Example 9-2. The check-expiry script

```
#!/bin/bash
expdate=$(date \
          --date $(whois "$1" \
                   | grep 'Registry Expiry Date:' \
                   | awk '{print $4}') \
          +'%Y-%m-%d')
echo "$expdate  $1"                 # Two values separated by a tab
```

Now, check all domains in the file *domains.txt* using a loop. Create a new script, `check-expiry-all`, shown in Example 9-3.

Example 9-3. The check-expiry-all script

```
#!/bin/bash
cat domains.txt | while read domain; do
   ./check-expiry "$domain"
   sleep 5                          # Be kind to the registrar's server
done
```

Run the script in the background, since it may take a while if you have many domains, and redirect all output (stdout and stderr) to a file:

```
$ ./check-expiry-all &> expiry.txt &
```

When the script finishes, the file *expiry.txt* contains the desired information:

```
$ cat expiry.txt
2022-08-13      example.com
2022-05-26      oreilly.com
2022-09-17      efficientlinux.com
⋮
```

Hooray! But don't stop there. The file *expiry.txt* is itself nicely structured for further processing, with two tabbed columns. For example, sort the dates and find the next domain to renew:

```
$ sort -n expiry.txt | head -n1
2022-05-26      oreilly.com
```

Or, use awk to find domains that have expired or are expiring today—that is, their expiration date (field 1) is less than or equal to today's date (printed with date +%Y-%m-%d):

```
$ awk "\$1<=\"$(date +%Y-%m-%d)\"" expiry.txt
```

A few notes on the preceding awk command:

- I escaped the dollar sign (before $1) and the double quotes around the date string so the shell doesn't evaluate them before awk can.

- I've cheated a bit by using the string operator <= to compare dates. It's not a mathematical comparison, just a string comparison, but it works because the date format, *YYYY-MM-DD*, sorts alphabetically and chronologically in the same order.

With more effort, you could do date math in awk to report expiration dates, say, two weeks in advance, then create a scheduled job to run the script nightly and email you a report. Feel free to experiment. The point here, however, is that once again, with a handful of commands, you've built a useful utility that's driven by a text file.

Building an Area Code Database

The next example uses a file with three fields that you can process in many ways. The file, named *areacodes.txt*, contains telephone area codes for the United States. Retrieve one from this book's supplemental material (*https://efficientlinux.com/exam ples*) in the directory *chapter09/build_area_code_database*, or create your own file, say, from Wikipedia (*https://oreil.ly/yz2M1*):[2]

```
201     NJ      Hackensack, Jersey City
202     DC      Washington
```

---

[2] The official list of area codes in CSV format (*https://oreil.ly/SptWL*), maintained by the North American Numbering Plan Administrator, lacks city names.

```
203    CT     New Haven, Stamford
⋮
989    MI     Saginaw
```

 Arrange the fields with predictable lengths first, so columns appear neatly lined up to the eye. Look how messy the file appears if you put the city names in the first column:

```
Hackensack, Jersey City 201     NJ
Washington       202     DC
⋮
```

Once this file is in place, you can do a lot with it. Look up area codes by state with grep, adding the -w option to match full words only (in case other text coincidentally contains "NJ"):

```
$ grep -w NJ areacodes.txt
201    NJ     Hackensack, Jersey City
551    NJ     Hackensack, Jersey City
609    NJ     Atlantic City, Trenton, southeast and central west
⋮
```

or look up cities by area code:

```
$ grep -w 202 areacodes.txt
202    DC     Washington
```

or by any string in the file:

```
$ grep Washing areacodes.txt
202    DC     Washington
227    MD     Silver Spring, Washington suburbs, Frederick
240    MD     Silver Spring, Washington suburbs, Frederick
⋮
```

Count the area codes with wc:

```
$ wc -l areacodes.txt
375 areacodes.txt
```

Find the state with the most area codes (the winner is California with 38):

```
$ cut -f2 areacodes.txt | sort | uniq -c | sort -nr | head -n1
     38 CA
```

Convert the file to CSV format to import into a spreadsheet application. Print the third field enclosed in double quotes to prevent its commas from being interpreted as CSV separator characters:

```
$ awk -F'\t' '{printf "%s,%s,\"%s\"\n", $1, $2, $3}' areacodes.txt \
  > areacodes.csv
$ head -n3 areacodes.csv
201,NJ,"Hackensack, Jersey City"
```

```
202,DC,"Washington"
203,CT,"New Haven, Stamford"
```

Collate all area codes for a given state onto a single line:

```
$ awk '$2~/^NJ$/{ac=ac FS $1} END {print "NJ:" ac}' areacodes.txt
NJ: 201 551 609 732 848 856 862 908 973
```

or collate for each state, using arrays and for loops as in "Improving the duplicate file detector" on page 88:

```
$ awk '{arr[$2]=arr[$2] " " $1} \
        END {for (i in arr) print i ":" arr[i]}' areacodes.txt \
  | sort
AB: 403 780
AK: 907
AL: 205 251 256 334 659
⋮
WY: 307
```

Turn any of the preceding commands into aliases, functions, or scripts, whatever is convenient. A simple example is the `areacode` script in Example 9-4.

Example 9-4. The areacode script

```
#!/bin/bash
if [ -n "$1" ]; then
  grep -iw "$1" areacodes.txt
fi
```

The `areacode` script searches for any whole word in the *areacodes.txt* file, such as an area code, state abbreviation, or city name:

```
$ areacode 617
617     MA      Boston
```

Building a Password Manager

For a final, in-depth example, let's store usernames, passwords, and notes in an encrypted text file, in a structured format for easy retrieval on the command line. The resulting command is a basic password manager, an application that eases the burden of memorizing lots of complicated passwords.

 Password management is a complex topic in computer security. This example creates an extremely basic password manager as an educational exercise. Don't use it for mission-critical applications.

The password file, named *vault*, has three fields separated by single tab characters:

- Username

- Password

- Notes (any text)

Create the *vault* file and add the data. The file is not encrypted yet, so insert only fake passwords for now:

```
$ touch vault                                Create an empty file
$ chmod 600 vault                            Set file permissions
$ emacs vault                                Edit the file
$ cat vault
sally    fake1    google.com account
ssmith   fake2    dropbox.com account for work
s999     fake3    Bank of America account, bankofamerica.com
smith2   fake4    My blog at wordpress.org
birdy    fake5    dropbox.com account for home
```

Store the vault in a known location:

```
$ mkdir ~/etc
$ mv vault ~/etc
```

The idea is to use a pattern-matching program like grep or awk to print lines that match a given string. This simple but powerful technique can match any part of any line, rather than just usernames or websites. For example:

```
$ cd ~/etc
$ grep sally vault                           Match a username
sally    fake1    google.com account
$ grep work vault                            Match the notes
ssmith   fake2    dropbox.com account for work
$ grep drop vault                            Match multiple lines
ssmith   fake2    dropbox.com account for work
birdy    fake5    dropbox.com account for home
```

Capture this simple functionality in a script; then, let's improve it step-by-step, including finally encrypting the *vault* file. Call the script pman for "password manager" and create the trivial version in Example 9-5.

Example 9-5. pman version 1: as simple as it gets

```
#!/bin/bash
# Just print matching lines
grep "$1" $HOME/etc/vault
```

Store the script in your search path:

```
$ chmod 700 pman
$ mv pman ~/bin
```

Try the script:

```
$ pman goog
sally   fake1   google.com account
$ pman account
sally   fake1   google.com account
ssmith  fake2   dropbox.com account for work
s999    fake3   Bank of America account, bankofamerica.com
birdy   fake5   dropbox.com account for home
$ pman facebook                                 (produces no output)
```

The next version in Example 9-6 adds a bit of error checking and some memorable variable names.

Example 9-6. pman version 2: add some error checking

```bash
#!/bin/bash
# Capture the script name.
# $0 is the path to the script, and basename prints the final filename.
PROGRAM=$(basename $0)
# Location of the password vault
DATABASE=$HOME/etc/vault

# Ensure that at least one argument was provided to the script.
# The expression >&2 directs echo to print on stderr instead of stdout.
if [ $# -ne 1 ]; then
    >&2 echo "$PROGRAM: look up passwords by string"
    >&2 echo "Usage: $PROGRAM string"
    exit 1
fi
# Store the first argument in a friendly, named variable
searchstring="$1"

# Search the vault and print an error message if nothing matches
grep "$searchstring" "$DATABASE"
if [ $? -ne 0 ]; then
    >&2 echo "$PROGRAM: no matches for '$searchstring'"
    exit 1
fi
```

Run the script:

```
$ pman
pman: look up passwords by string
Usage: pman string
$ pman smith
ssmith  fake2   dropbox.com account for work
smith2  fake4   My blog at wordpress.org
$ pman xyzzy
pman: no matches for 'xyzzy'
```

A shortcoming of this technique is that it won't scale. If *vault* contained hundreds of lines and grep matched and printed 63 of them, you'd have to hunt by eye to find the password you need. Improve the script by adding a unique key (a string) to each line in the third column, and update pman to search for that unique key first. The *vault* file, with third column bolded, now looks like:

```
sally    fake1   google  google.com account
ssmith   fake2   dropbox dropbox.com account for work
s999     fake3   bank    Bank of America account, bankofamerica.com
smith2   fake4   blog    My blog at wordpress.org
birdy    fake5   dropbox2        dropbox.com account for home
```

Example 9-7 shows the updated script that uses awk instead of grep. It also uses command substitution to capture the output and check if it's empty (the test -z means "zero length string"). Notice that if you search for a key that doesn't exist in *vault*, pman falls back to its original behavior and prints all lines that match the search string.

Example 9-7. pman version 3: prioritize searching for the key in the third column

```
#!/bin/bash
PROGRAM=$(basename $0)
DATABASE=$HOME/etc/vault

if [ $# -ne 1 ]; then
    >&2 echo "$PROGRAM: look up passwords"
    >&2 echo "Usage: $PROGRAM string"
    exit 1
fi
searchstring="$1"

# Look for exact matches in the third column
match=$(awk '$3~/^'$searchstring'$/' "$DATABASE")

# If the search string doesn't match a key, find all matches
if [ -z "$match" ]; then
    match=$(awk "/$searchstring/" "$DATABASE")
fi

# If still no match, print an error message and exit
if [ -z "$match" ]; then
    >&2 echo "$PROGRAM: no matches for '$searchstring'"
    exit 1
fi

# Print the match
echo "$match"
```

Run the script:

```
$ pman dropbox
ssmith  fake2    dropbox dropbox.com account for work
$ pman drop
ssmith  fake2    dropbox dropbox.com account for work
birdy   fake5    dropbox2        dropbox.com account for home
```

The plain-text file *vault* is a security risk, so encrypt it with the standard Linux encryption program GnuPG, which is invoked as gpg. If you already have GnuPG set up for use, that's great. Otherwise, set it up with the following command, supplying your email address:[3]

```
$ gpg --quick-generate-key your_email_address default default never
```

You're prompted for a passphrase for the key (twice). Provide a strong passphrase. When gpg completes, you're ready to encrypt the password file using public key encryption, producing the file *vault.gpg*:

```
$ cd ~/etc
$ gpg -e -r your_email_address vault
$ ls vault*
vault   vault.gpg
```

As a test, decrypt the *vault.gpg* file to stdout:[4]

```
$ gpg -d -q vault.gpg
Passphrase: xxxxxxxx
sally   fake1    google  google.com account
ssmith  fake2    dropbox dropbox.com account for work
⋮
```

Next, update your script to use the encrypted *vault.gpg* file instead of the plain-text *vault* file. That means decrypting *vault.gpg* to stdout and piping its contents to awk for matching, as in Example 9-8.

Example 9-8. pman version 4: using an encrypted vault

```
#!/bin/bash
PROGRAM=$(basename $0)
# Use the encrypted file
DATABASE=$HOME/etc/vault.gpg

if [ $# -ne 1 ]; then
    >&2 echo "$PROGRAM: look up passwords"
    >&2 echo "Usage: $PROGRAM string"
```

---

3 This command generates a public/private key pair with all default options and an expiration date of "never." To learn more, see man gpg to read about gpg options, or seek out a GnuPG tutorial online.

4 If gpg proceeds without prompting for your passphrase, it has cached (saved) your passphrase temporarily.

```
        exit 1
fi
searchstring="$1"

# Store the decrypted text in a variable
decrypted=$(gpg -d -q "$DATABASE")
# Look for exact matches in the third column
match=$(echo "$decrypted" | awk '$3~/^'$searchstring'$/')

# If the search string doesn't match a key, find all matches
if [ -z "$match" ]; then
    match=$(echo "$decrypted" | awk "/$searchstring/")
fi

# If still no match, print an error message and exit
if [ -z "$match" ]; then
    >&2 echo "$PROGRAM: no matches for '$searchstring'"
    exit 1
fi

# Print the match
echo "$match"
```

The script now displays passwords from the encrypted file:

```
$ pman dropbox
Passphrase: xxxxxxxx
ssmith  fake2   dropbox dropbox.com account for work
$ pman drop
Passphrase: xxxxxxxx
ssmith  fake2   dropbox dropbox.com account for work
birdy   fake5   dropbox2        dropbox.com account for home
```

All the pieces are in place now for your password manager. Some final steps are:

- When you're convinced that you can decrypt the *vault.gpg* file reliably, delete the original *vault* file.

- If you wish, replace the fake passwords with real ones. See "Editing Encrypted Files Directly" on page 166 for advice on editing an encrypted text file.

- Support comments in the password vault—lines that begin with a pound sign (#) —so you can make notes about the entries. To do so, update the script to pipe the decrypted contents to grep -v to filter any lines that begin with a pound sign:

  ```
  decrypted=$(gpg -d -q "$DATABASE" | grep -v '^#')
  ```

Printing passwords on stdout isn't great for security. "Improving the Password Manager" on page 186 will update this script to copy and paste passwords instead of printing them.

Editing Encrypted Files Directly

To modify an encrypted file, the most direct, tedious, and insecure method is to decrypt the file, edit it, and re-encrypt it.

```
$ cd ~/etc
$ gpg vault.gpg                              Decrypt
Passphrase: xxxxxxxx
$ emacs vault                                Use your favorite text editor
$ gpg -e -r your_email_address vault         Encrypt for yourself
$ rm vault
```

For easier editing of the *vault.gpg* file, both emacs and vim have modes for editing GnuPG-encrypted files. Begin by adding this line to a bash configuration file and sourcing it in any associated shells:

```
export GPG_TTY=$(tty)
```

For emacs, set up the EasyPG package, which is built-in. Add the following lines to the configuration file *$HOME/.emacs* and restart emacs. Replace the string *GnuPG ID here* with the email address associated with your key, such as smith@example.com:

```
(load-library "pinentry")
(setq epa-pinentry-mode 'loopback)
(setq epa-file-encrypt-to "GnuPG ID here")
(pinentry-start)
```

Then edit any encrypted file, and emacs prompts for your passphrase and decrypts it into a buffer for editing. On save, emacs encrypts the contents of the buffer.

For vim, try the plugin vim-gnupg (*https://oreil.ly/mnwYc*) and add these lines to the configuration file *$HOME/.vimrc*:

```
let g:GPGPreferArmor=1
let g:GPGDefaultRecipients=["GnuPG ID here"]
```

Consider creating an alias to edit the password vault conveniently, using the technique from the section "Edit Frequently Edited Files with an Alias" on page 52:

```
alias pwedit="$EDITOR $HOME/etc/vault.gpg"
```

Summary

File paths, domain names, area codes, and login credentials are just a few examples of data that work well in a structured text file. How about:

- Your music files? (Use a Linux command like id3tool to extract ID3 information from your MP3 files and place it into a file.)
- The contacts on your mobile device? (Use an app to export the contacts to CSV format, upload them to cloud storage, and then download them to your Linux machine for processing.)
- Your grades in school? (Use awk to track your grade point average.)
- A list of movies you've seen or books you've read, with additional data (ratings, authors, actors, etc.)?

In this manner, you can build an ecosystem of time-saving commands that are personally meaningful or productive for work, limited only by your imagination.

## PART III

Extra Goodies

The final chapters dive into specialized topics: some in detail and others just briefly to whet your appetite to learn more.

## CHAPTER 10

Efficiency at the Keyboard

On a typical day, on a typical Linux workstation, you might have many application windows open: web browsers, text editors, software development environments, music players, video editors, virtual machines, and so on. Some applications are GUI-focused, such as a paint program, and tailored to a pointing device like a mouse or trackball. Others are more keyboard-focused, like a shell inside a terminal program. A typical Linux user might shift between keyboard and mouse dozens (or even hundreds) of times per hour. Each switch takes time. It slows you down. If you can reduce the number of switches, you can work more efficiently.

This chapter is about spending more time at the keyboard and less with a pointing device. Ten fingers tapping one hundred keys are often more nimble than a couple of fingers on a mouse. I'm not just talking about using keyboard shortcuts—I'm confident you can look them up without needing this book (though I present a few). I'm talking about a different approach to speed up some everyday tasks that seem inherently "mousey": working with windows, retrieving information from the web, and copying and pasting with the clipboard.

Working with Windows

In this section, I share tips for launching windows efficiently, particularly shell windows (terminals) and browser windows.

Instant Shells and Browsers

Most Linux desktop environments, such as GNOME, KDE Plasma, Unity, and Cinnamon, provide some way to define hotkeys or custom keyboard shortcuts—special keystrokes that launch commands or perform other operations. I strongly recommend that you define keyboard shortcuts for these common operations:

- Opening a new shell window (a terminal program)
- Opening a new web browser window

With these shortcuts defined, you can open a terminal or browser anytime in an instant, no matter what other application you're in the middle of using.[1] To set this up, you need to know the following:

The command that launches your preferred terminal program
> Some popular ones are gnome-terminal, konsole, and xterm.

The command that launches your preferred browser
> Some popular ones are firefox, google-chrome, and opera.

How to define a custom keyboard shortcut
> The instructions differ for each desktop environment and may change from version to version, so it's better if you look them up on the web. Search for the name of your desktop environment followed by "define keyboard shortcut."

On my desktop, I assign the keyboard shortcut Ctrl-Windows-T to run konsole and Ctrl-Windows-C to run google-chrome.

Working Directories

When you launch a shell via a keyboard shortcut in your desktop environment, it's a child of your login shell. Its current directory is your home directory (unless you've somehow configured it to be different).

Contrast this with opening a new shell from within your terminal program—by explicitly running (say) gnome-terminal or xterm at the command line or using your terminal program's menu to open a new window. In this case, the new shell is a child of *that terminal's shell*. Its current directory is the same as its parent's, which might not be your home directory.

One-Shot Windows

Suppose you're in the middle of using several applications when suddenly you need a shell to run one command. Many users would grab the mouse and hunt through their open windows for a running terminal. Don't do this—you're wasting time. Just pop open a new terminal with your hotkey, run your command, and exit the terminal right afterward.

---

1 Unless you're working in an application that captures all keystrokes, such as a virtual machine in a window.

Once you have hotkeys assigned to launch terminal programs and browser windows, go ahead and open and close these windows in great numbers with wild abandon. I recommend it! Create and destroy terminals and browser windows on a regular basis, rather than leaving them open for a long time. I call these short-lived windows *one-shot windows*. You pop them open quickly, use them for a few moments, and close them.

You might leave a few shells open for a long time if you're developing software or performing other lengthy work, but one-shot terminal windows are perfect for other random commands throughout the day. *It's often quicker to pop up a new terminal than to search your screen for an existing terminal.* Don't ask yourself, "Where's that terminal window I need?" and poke around the desktop looking for it. Make a new one and close it after it has served its purpose.

Likewise for web browser windows. Do you ever lift your head after a long day of Linux hacking to discover that your browser has just one window and 83 open tabs? That's a symptom of too few one-shot windows. Pop one open, view whatever web page you need to view, and close it. Need to revisit the page later? Locate it in your browser history.

Browser Keyboard Shortcuts

While we're on the topic of browser windows, make sure you know the most important keyboard shortcuts in Table 10-1. If your hands are already on the keyboard and you want to browse to a new website, it's often faster to press Ctrl-L to jump to the address bar or Ctrl-T to open a tab than to point and click.

Table 10-1. The most important keyboard shortcuts for Firefox, Google Chrome, and Opera

Action	Keyboard shortcut
Open new window	Ctrl-N
Open new private/incognito window	Ctrl-Shift-P (Firefox), Ctrl-Shift-N (Chrome and Opera)
Open new tab	Ctrl-T
Close tab	Ctrl-W
Cycle through browser tabs	Ctrl-Tab (cycle forward) and Ctrl-Shift-Tab (cycle backward)
Jump to address bar	Ctrl-L (or Alt-D or F6)
Find (search) for text in current page	Ctrl-F
Display your browsing history	Ctrl-H

Switching Windows and Desktops

When your busy desktop is filled with windows, how do you find the window you want quickly? You could point and click your way through the morass, but it's often quicker to use the keyboard shortcut Alt-Tab. Keep pressing Alt-Tab and you cycle through all windows on the desktop, one at a time. When you reach the window you want, release the keys and that window is in focus and ready to use. To cycle in the reverse direction, press Alt-Shift-Tab.

To cycle through all windows on the desktop that belong to the same application, such as all Firefox windows, press Alt-` (Alt-backquote, or Alt plus the key above Tab). To cycle backward, add the Shift key (Alt-Shift-backquote).

Once you can switch windows, it's time to talk about switching desktops. If you do serious work on Linux and you're using just one desktop, you're missing out on a great way to organize your work. Multiple desktops, also called workspaces or virtual desktops, are just what they sound like. Instead of a single desktop, you might have four or six or more, each with its own windows, and you can switch between them.

On my workstation running Ubuntu Linux with KDE Plasma, I run six virtual desktops and assign them different purposes. Desktop #1 is my main workspace with email and browsing, #2 is for family-related tasks, #3 is where I run VMware virtual machines, #4 is for writing books like this one, and #5–6 are for any ad hoc tasks. These consistent assignments make it quick and easy to locate my open windows from different applications.

Each Linux desktop environment such as GNOME, KDE Plasma, Cinnamon, and Unity has its own way to implement virtual desktops, and they all provide a graphical "switcher" or "pager" to switch between them. I recommend defining keyboard shortcuts in your desktop environment to jump speedily to each desktop. On my computer, I defined Windows + F1 through Windows + F6 to jump to desktops #1 through #6, respectively.

There are many other styles of working with desktops and windows. Some people use one desktop per application: a desktop for shells, a desktop for web browsing, a desktop for word processing, and so on. Some people with small laptop screens open just one window on each desktop, full-screen, instead of multiple windows per desktop. Find a style that works for you, as long as it's speedy and efficient.

Web Access from the Command Line

Point-and-click browsers are almost synonymous with the web, but you can also access websites from the Linux command line to great effect.

Launching Browser Windows from the Command Line

You may be accustomed to launching a web browser by clicking or tapping an icon, but you can also do it from the Linux command line. If the browser isn't running yet, add an ampersand to run it in the background so you get your shell prompt back:

```
$ firefox &
$ google-chrome &
$ opera &
```

If a given browser is already running, omit the ampersand. The command tells an existing browser instance to open a new window or tab. The command immediately exits and gives you the shell prompt back.

 A backgrounded browser command might print diagnostic messages and clutter up your shell window. To prevent this, redirect all output to *dev/null* when you first launch the browser. For example:

```
$ firefox &> /dev/null &
```

To open a browser and visit a URL from the command line, provide the URL as an argument:

```
$ firefox https://oreilly.com
$ google-chrome https://oreilly.com
$ opera https://oreilly.com
```

By default, the preceding commands open a new tab and bring it into focus. To force them to open a new window instead, add an option:

```
$ firefox --new-window https://oreilly.com
$ google-chrome --new-window https://oreilly.com
$ opera --new-window https://oreilly.com
```

To open a private or incognito browser window, add the appropriate command-line option:

```
$ firefox --private-window https://oreilly.com
$ google-chrome --incognito https://oreilly.com
$ opera --private https://oreilly.com
```

The preceding commands might seem like a lot of typing and effort, but you can be efficient by defining aliases for sites you visit often:

```
# Place in a shell configuration file and source it:
alias oreilly="firefox --new-window https://oreilly.com"
```

Likewise, if you have a file that contains a URL of interest, extract the URL with `grep`, `cut`, or other Linux commands and pass it to the browser on the command line with command substitution. Here's an example with a tab-separated file with two columns:

```
$ cat urls.txt
duckduckgo.com  My search engine
nytimes.com     My newspaper
spotify.com     My music
$ grep music urls.txt | cut -f1
spotify.com
$ google-chrome https://$(grep music urls.txt | cut -f1)        Visit spotify
```

Or, suppose you keep track of packages you're expecting with a file of tracking numbers:

```
$ cat packages.txt
1Z0EW7360669374701        UPS     Shoes
568733462924              FedEx   Kitchen blender
9305510823011761842873    USPS    Care package from Mom
```

The shell script in Example 10-1 opens the tracking pages for the appropriate shippers (UPS, FedEx, or the US Postal Service) by appending tracking numbers to the appropriate URLs.

Example 10-1. track-it script that hits the tracking page of shippers

```
#!/bin/bash
PROGRAM=$(basename $0)
DATAFILE=packages.txt
# Choose a browser command: firefox, opera, google-chrome
BROWSER="opera"
errors=0

cat "$DATAFILE" | while read line; do
  track=$(echo "$line" | awk '{print $1}')
  service=$(echo "$line" | awk '{print $2}')
  case "$service" in
    UPS)
      $BROWSER "https://www.ups.com/track?tracknum=$track" &
      ;;
    FedEx)
      $BROWSER "https://www.fedex.com/fedextrack/?trknbr=$track" &
      ;;
    USPS)
      $BROWSER "https://tools.usps.com/go/TrackConfirmAction?tLabels=$track" &
      ;;
    *)
      >&2 echo "$PROGRAM: Unknown service '$service'"
      errors=1
      ;;
  esac
done
exit $errors
```

Retrieving HTML with curl and wget

Web browsers aren't the only Linux programs that visit websites. The programs `curl` and `wget` can download web pages and other web content with a single command, without touching a browser. By default, `curl` prints its output to stdout, and `wget` saves its output to a file (after printing lots of diagnostic messages):

```
$ curl https://efficientlinux.com/welcome.html
Welcome to Efficient Linux.com!
$ wget https://efficientlinux.com/welcome.html
--2021-10-27 20:05:47--  https://efficientlinux.com/
Resolving efficientlinux.com (efficientlinux.com)...
Connecting to efficientlinux.com (efficientlinux.com)...
⋮
2021-10-27 20:05:47 (12.8 MB/s) - 'welcome.html' saved [32/32]
$ cat welcome.html
Welcome to Efficient Linux.com!
```

Some sites don't support retrieval by `wget` and `curl`. Both commands can masquerade as another browser in such cases. Just tell each program to change its user agent—the string that identifies a web client to a web server. A convenient user agent is "Mozilla":

```
$ wget -U Mozilla url
$ curl -A Mozilla url
```

Both `wget` and `curl` have tons of options and features that you can discover on their manpages. For now, let's see how to incorporate these commands into brash one-liners. Suppose the website *efficientlinux.com* has a directory, *images*, containing files *1.jpg* through *20.jpg*, and you'd like to download them. Their URLs are:

```
https://efficientlinux.com/images/1.jpg
https://efficientlinux.com/images/2.jpg
https://efficientlinux.com/images/3.jpg
⋮
```

An inefficient method would be to visit each URL in a web browser, one at a time, and download each image. (Raise your hand if you've ever done this!) A better method is to use `wget`. Generate the URLs with `seq` and `awk`:

```
$ seq 1 20 | awk '{print "https://efficientlinux.com/images/" $1 ".jpg"}'
https://efficientlinux.com/images/1.jpg
https://efficientlinux.com/images/2.jpg
https://efficientlinux.com/images/3.jpg
⋮
```

Then add the string "wget" into the awk program and pipe the resulting commands to bash for execution:

```
$ seq 1 20 \
  | awk '{print "wget https://efficientlinux.com/images/" $1 ".jpg"}' \
  | bash
```

Alternatively, use xargs to create and execute the wget commands:

```
$ seq 1 20 | xargs -I@ wget https://efficientlinux.com/images/@.jpg
```

The xargs solution is superior if your wget commands contain any special characters. The "pipe to bash" solution would cause the shell to evaluate those characters (which you don't want to happen) whereas xargs would not.

My example was a bit contrived because the image filenames are so uniform. In a more realistic example, you could download all the images on a web page by retrieving the page with curl, piping it through a clever sequence of commands to isolate the image URLs, one per line, and then applying one of the techniques I just showed you:

```
curl URL | ...clever pipeline here... | xargs -n1 wget
```

Processing HTML with HTML-XML-utils

If you know some HTML and CSS, you can parse the HTML source of web pages from the command line. It's sometimes more efficient than copying and pasting chunks of a web page from a browser window by hand. A handy suite of tools for this purpose is HTML-XML-utils, which is available in many Linux distros and from the World Wide Web Consortium (*https://oreil.ly/81yM2*). A general recipe is:

1. Use curl (or wget) to capture the HTML source.
2. Use hxnormalize to help ensure that the HTML is well-formed.
3. Identify CSS selectors for the values you want to capture.
4. Use hxselect to isolate the values, and pipe the output to further commands for processing.

Let's extend the example from "Building an Area Code Database" on page 158 to grab area code data from the web and produce the *areacodes.txt* file used in that example. For your convenience, I've created an HTML table of area codes for you to download and process, shown in Figure 10-1.

Area code	State	Location
201	NJ	Hackensack, Jersey City
202	DC	Washington
203	CT	New Haven, Stamford
204	MB	entire province
205	AL	Birmingham, Tuscaloosa
206	WA	Seattle
207	ME	entire state
208	ID	entire state
209	CA	Modesto, Stockton
210	TX	San Antonio
212	NY	New York City, Manhattan

Figure 10-1. A table of area codes at https://efficientlinux.com/areacodes.html

First, grab the HTML source with `curl`, using the `-s` option to suppress on-screen messages. Pipe the output to `hxnormalize -x` to clean it up a bit. Pipe it to `less` to view the output one screenful at a time:

```
$ curl -s https://efficientlinux.com/areacodes.html \
  | hxnormalize -x \
  | less
<!DOCTYPE HTML PUBLIC "-//W3C//DTD HTML 4.01//EN"
"http://www.w3.org/TR/html4/strict.dtd">
<html>
  ⋮
  <body>
    <h1>Area code test</h1>
    ⋮
```

The HTML table on that page, shown in Example 10-2, has CSS ID #ac, and its three columns (area code, state, and location) use CSS classes `ac`, `state`, and `cities`, respectively.

Example 10-2. Partial HTML source of the table in Figure 10-1

```
<table id="ac">
  <thead>
    <tr>
      <th>Area code</th>
      <th>State</th>
      <th>Location</th>
    </tr>
```

```
    </thead>
    <tbody>
      <tr>
        <td class="ac">201</td>
        <td class="state">NJ</td>
        <td class="cities">Hackensack, Jersey City</td>
      </tr>
      ⋮
</tbody>
</table>
```

Run `hxselect` to extract the area code data from each table cell, supplying the `-c` option to omit the `td` tags from the output. Print the results as one long line, with fields separated by a character of your choice (using the `-s` option).[2] I chose the character @ for its easy visibility on the page:

```
$ curl -s https://efficientlinux.com/areacodes.html \
  | hxnormalize -x \
  | hxselect -c -s@ '#ac .ac, #ac .state, #ac .cities'
201@NJ@Hackensack, Jersey City@202@DC@Washington@203@CT@New Haven, Stamford@...
```

Finally, pipe the output to `sed` to turn this long line into three tab-separated columns. Write a regular expression to match the following strings:

1. An area code, which consists of digits, `[0-9]*`

2. An @ symbol

3. A state abbreviation, which is two capital letters, `[A-Z][A-Z]`

4. An @ symbol

5. The cities, which is any text that doesn't include an @ symbol, `[^@]*`

6. An @ symbol

Combine the parts to produce the following regular expression:

```
[0-9]*@[A-Z][A-Z]@[^@]*@
```

Capture the area code, state, and cities as three subexpressions by surrounding them with `\(` and `\)`. You now have a complete regular expression for `sed`:

```
\([0-9]*\)@\([A-Z][A-Z]\)@\([^@]*\)@
```

For `sed`'s replacement string, provide the three subexpressions separated by tabs and terminated by newlines, which produces the format of the *areacodes.txt* file:

---

2 This example uses three CSS selectors, but some old versions of `hxselect` can handle only two. If your version of `hxselect` is afflicted by this shortcoming, download the latest version from the World Wide Web Consortium (*https://oreil.ly/81yM2*) and build it with the command `configure && make`.

```
\1\t\2\t\3\n
```

Combine the preceding regular expression and replacement string to make this sed
script:

```
s/\([0-9]*\)@\([A-Z][A-Z]\)@\([^@]*\)@/\1\t\2\t\3\n/g
```

The finished command produces the needed data for the *areacodes.txt* file:

```
$ curl -s https://efficientlinux.com/areacodes.html \
  | hxnormalize -x \
  | hxselect -c -s'@' '#ac .ac, #ac .state, #ac .cities' \
  | sed 's/\([0-9]*\)@\([A-Z][A-Z]\)@\([^@]*\)@/\1\t\2\t\3\n/g'
201     NJ      Hackensack, Jersey City
202     DC      Washington
203     CT      New Haven, Stamford
⋮
```

Handling Long Regular Expressions

If your sed scripts become so long they look like random noise:

```
s/\([0-9]*\)@\([A-Z][A-Z]\)@\([^@]*\)@/\1\t\2\t\3\n/g
```

try splitting them up. Store parts of the regular expression in several shell variables,
and combine the variables later, as in the following shell script:

```
# The three parts of the regular expression.
# Use single quotes to prevent evaluation by the shell.
areacode='\([0-9]*\)'
state='\([A-Z][A-Z]\)'
cities='\([^@]*\)'

# Combine the three parts, separated by @ symbols.
# Use double quotes to permit variable evaluation by the shell.
regexp="$areacode@$state@$cities@"

# The replacement string.
# Use single quotes to prevent evaluation by the shell.
replacement='\1\t\2\t\3\n'

# The sed script now becomes much simpler to read:
#   s/$regexp/$replacement/g
# Run the full command:
curl -s https://efficientlinux.com/areacodes.html \
  | hxnormalize -x \
  | hxselect -c -s'@' '#ac .ac, #ac .state, #ac .cities' \
  | sed "s/$regexp/$replacement/g"
```

Retrieving Rendered Web Content with a Text-Based Browser

Sometimes when you retrieve data from the web at the command line, you might not want the HTML source of a web page, but a rendered version of the page in text. The rendered text might be easier to parse. To accomplish this task, use a text-based browser such as `lynx` or `links`. Text-based browsers display web pages in a stripped-down format without images or other fancy features. Figure 10-2 displays the area codes page from the previous section as rendered by `lynx`.

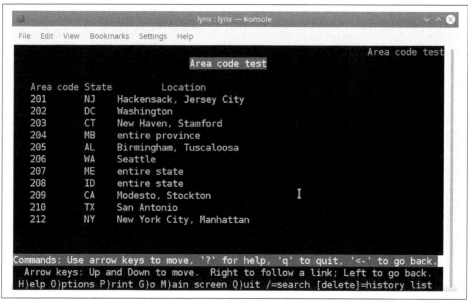

Figure 10-2. lynx renders the page https://efficientlinux.com/areacodes.html

Both `lynx` and `links` download a rendered page with the `-dump` option. Use whichever program you prefer.

```
$ lynx -dump https://efficientlinux.com/areacodes.html > tempfile
$ cat tempfile
                      Area code test

Area code State   Location
201        NJ      Hackensack, Jersey City
202        DC      Washington
203        CT      New Haven, Stamford
⋮
```

lynx and links are also great for checking out a suspicious-looking link when you're unsure if it's legitimate or malicious. These text-based browsers don't support JavaScript or render images, so they are less vulnerable to attack. (They can't promise complete security, of course, so use your best judgment.)

Clipboard Control from the Command Line

Every modern software application with an Edit menu includes the operations cut, copy, and paste to transfer content in and out of the system clipboard. You might also know keyboard shortcuts for these operations. But did you know that you can process the clipboard directly from the command line?

A bit of background first: copy and paste operations on Linux are part of a more general mechanism called *X selections*. A selection is a destination for copied content, such as the system clipboard. "X" is just the name of the Linux windowing software.

Most Linux desktop environments that are built on X, such as GNOME, Unity, Cinnamon, and KDE Plasma, support two selections.[3] The first is the *clipboard*, and it works just like clipboards on other operating systems. When you run cut or copy operations in an application, the content goes to the clipboard, and you retrieve the content with a paste operation. A less familiar X selection is called the *primary selection*. When you select text in certain applications, it's written to the primary selection even if you don't run a copy operation. An example is highlighting text in a terminal window with the mouse. That text is automatically written to the primary selection.

If you connect to a Linux host remotely by SSH or similar programs, copy/paste generally is handled by the local computer, not by X selections on the remote Linux host.

Table 10-2 lists mouse and keyboard operations to access X selections in GNOME's Terminal (gnome-terminal) and KDE's Konsole (konsole). If you use a different terminal program, check its Edit menu for keyboard equivalents for Copy and Paste.

---

3 Really there are three X selections, but one of them, called the *secondary selection*, is rarely exposed by modern desktop environments.

Table 10-2. Accessing X selections in common terminal programs

Operation	Clipboard	Primary selection
Copy (mouse)	Open the right button menu and select Copy	Click and drag; or double-click to select the current word; or triple-click to select the current line
Paste (mouse)	Open the right button menu and select Paste	Press the middle mouse button (usually the scroll wheel)
Copy (keyboard)	Ctrl-Shift-C	*n/a*
Paste (keyboard), gnome-terminal	Ctrl-Shift-V or Ctrl-Shift-Insert	Shift-Insert
Paste (keyboard), konsole	Ctrl-Shift-V or Shift-Insert	Ctrl-Shift-Insert

Connecting Selections to stdin and stdout

Linux provides a command, xclip, that connects X selections to stdin and stdout. You can therefore insert copy and paste operations into pipelines and other combined commands. For example, you may have copied text into an application like this:

1. Run a Linux command and redirect its output to a file.

2. View the file.

3. Use your mouse to copy the file's content to the clipboard.

4. Paste the content into another application.

With xclip, you can shorten the process considerably:

1. Pipe a Linux command's output to xclip.

2. Paste the content into another application.

Conversely, you may have pasted text into a file to process it with Linux commands like this:

1. Use your mouse to copy a bunch of text in an application program.

2. Paste it into a text file.

3. Process the text file with Linux commands.

With xclip -o, you can skip the intermediate text file:

1. Use your mouse to copy a bunch of text in an application program.

2. Pipe the output of xclip -o to other Linux commands for processing.

If you're reading this book digitally on a Linux device and want to try some of the xclip commands in this section, *don't copy and paste the commands* into a shell window. Type the commands by hand. Why? Because your copy operation may overwrite the same X selection that the commands access with xclip, causing the commands to produce unexpected results.

By default, xclip reads stdin and writes the primary selection. It can read from a file:

```
$ xclip < myfile.txt
```

or from a pipe:

```
$ echo "Efficient Linux at the Command Line" | xclip
```

Now print the text to stdout, or pipe the selection contents to other commands, such as wc:

```
$ xclip -o                              Paste to stdout
Efficient Linux at the Command Line
$ xclip -o > anotherfile.txt            Paste to a file
$ xclip -o | wc -w                      Count words
6
```

Any combined command that writes to stdout can pipe its results to xclip, like this one from "Command #6: uniq" on page 14:

```
$ cut -f1 grades | sort | uniq -c | sort -nr | head -n1 | cut -c9 | xclip
```

Clear the primary selection by setting its value to the empty string with echo -n:

```
$ echo -n | xclip
```

The -n option is important; otherwise, echo prints a newline character on stdout that ends up in the primary selection.

To copy text to the clipboard instead of the primary selection, run xclip with the option -selection clipboard:

```
$ echo https://oreilly.com | xclip -selection clipboard        Copy
$ xclip -selection clipboard -o                                Paste
https://oreilly.com
```

xclip options may be abbreviated as long as they're unambiguous:

```
$ xclip -sel c -o              Same as xclip -selection clipboard -o
https://oreilly.com
```

Launch a Firefox browser window to visit the preceding URL, using command substitution:

```
$ firefox $(xclip -selection clipboard -o)
```

Linux offers another command, xsel, that also reads and writes X selections. It has a few extra features, like clearing a selection (xsel -c) and appending to a selection (xsel -a). Feel free to read the manpage and experiment with xsel.

Improving the Password Manager

Let's use your newfound knowledge of xclip to integrate X selections into the password manager pman from "Building a Password Manager" on page 160. When the modified pman script matches a single line in the *vault.gpg* file, it writes the username to the clipboard and the password to the primary selection. Afterward, you can fill out a login page on the web, for example, by pasting the username with Ctrl-V and pasting the password with the middle mouse button.

 Ensure that you are *not* running a clipboard manager or any other applications that keep track of X selections and their contents. Otherwise, usernames and/or passwords become visible in the clipboard manager, which is a security risk.

The new version of pman is in Example 10-3. pman's behavior has changed in the following ways:

- A new function, load_password, loads the associated username and password into X selections.

- If pman locates a single match for the search string, either by key (field 3) or by any other part of a line, it runs load_password.

- If pman locates multiple matches, it prints all the keys and notes (fields 3 and 4) from the matching lines so the user can search again by key.

Example 10-3. An improved pman script that loads username and password as selections

```
#!/bin/bash
PROGRAM=$(basename $0)
DATABASE=$HOME/etc/vault.gpg

load_password () {
    # Place username (field 1) into clipboard
    echo "$1" | cut -f1 | tr -d '\n' | xclip -selection clipboard
    # Place password (field 2) into X primary selection
    echo "$1" | cut -f2 | tr -d '\n' | xclip -selection primary
    # Give feedback to the user
    echo "$PROGRAM: Found" $(echo "$1" | cut -f3- --output-delimiter ': ')
    echo "$PROGRAM: username and password loaded into X selections"
}
```

```
if [ $# -ne 1 ]; then
    >&2 echo "$PROGRAM: look up passwords"
    >&2 echo "Usage: $PROGRAM string"
    exit 1
fi
searchstring="$1"

# Store the decrypted text in a variable
decrypted=$(gpg -d -q "$DATABASE")
if [ $? -ne 0 ]; then
    >&2 echo "$PROGRAM: could not decrypt $DATABASE"
    exit 1
fi

# Look for exact matches in the third column
match=$(echo "$decrypted" | awk '$3~/^'$searchstring'$/')
if [ -n "$match" ]; then
    load_password "$match"
    exit $?
fi

# Look for any match
match=$(echo "$decrypted" | awk "/$searchstring/")
if [ -z "$match" ]; then
    >&2 echo "$PROGRAM: no matches"
    exit 1
fi

# Count the matches
count=$(echo "$match" | wc -l)

case "$count" in
    0)
        >&2 echo "$PROGRAM: no matches"
        exit 1
        ;;
    1)
        load_password "$match"
        exit $?
        ;;
    *)
        >&2 echo "$PROGRAM: multiple matches for the following keys:"
        echo "$match" | cut -f3
        >&2 echo "$PROGRAM: rerun this script with one of the keys"
        exit
        ;;
esac
```

Run the script:

```
$ pman dropbox
Passphrase: xxxxxxxx
pman: Found dropbox: dropbox.com account for work
pman: username and password loaded into X selections
$ pman account
Passphrase: xxxxxxxx
pman: multiple matches for the following keys:
google
dropbox
bank
dropbox2
pman: rerun this script with one of the keys
```

Passwords hang around in the primary selection until it's overwritten. To automatically clear the password after (say) 30 seconds, append the following line to the load_password function. The line launches a subshell in the background that waits 30 seconds and then clears the primary selection (by setting it to the empty string). Adjust the number 30 as you see fit.

```
(sleep 30 && echo -n | xclip -selection primary) &
```

If you defined a custom keyboard shortcut to launch terminal windows in "Instant Shells and Browsers" on page 171, you now have a quick way to access your passwords. Pop up a terminal by hotkey, run pman, and close the terminal.

Summary

I hope this chapter has encouraged you to try some new techniques that keep your hands on the keyboard. They may seem effortful at first, but with practice they become quick and automatic. Soon you'll be the envy of your Linux friends as you smoothly manipulate desktop windows, web content, and X selections in ways that the mouse-bound masses cannot.

## CHAPTER 11

Final Time-Savers

I've had a lot of fun writing this book, and I hope you've had fun reading it too. For the last act, let's cover a bunch of smaller topics that didn't quite fit into the earlier chapters. These topics have made me a better Linux user, and maybe they'll help you as well.

Quick Wins

The following time-savers are simple to learn in a few minutes.

Jumping Into Your Editor from less

When you're viewing a text file with `less` and want to edit the file, don't exit `less`. Just press v to launch your preferred text editor. It loads the file and places the cursor right at the spot you were viewing in `less`. Exit the editor and you're back in `less` at the original location.

For this trick to work best, set the environment variable `EDITOR` and/or `VISUAL` to an editing command. These environment variables represent your default Linux text editor that may be launched by various commands, including `less`, `lynx`, `git`, `crontab`, and numerous email programs. For example, to set `emacs` as your default editor, place either of the following lines (or both) in a shell configuration file and source it:

```
VISUAL=emacs
EDITOR=emacs
```

If you don't set these variables, your default editor is whatever your Linux system sets it to be, which is usually `vim`. If you end up inside of `vim` and you don't know how to use it, don't panic. Quit `vim` by pressing the Escape key and typing `:q!` (a colon, the letter *q*, and an exclamation point), then press Enter. To quit emacs, press Ctrl-X followed by Ctrl-C.

Editing Files That Contain a Given String

Want to edit every file in the current directory that contains a certain string (or regular expression)? Generate a list of filenames with grep -l and pass them to your editor with command substitution. Assuming your editor is vim, the command is as follows:

```
$ vim $(grep -l string *)
```

Edit all files containing *string* in an entire directory tree (current directory and all subdirectories) by adding the -r option (recursive) to grep and beginning in the current directory (the dot):

```
$ vim $(grep -lr string .)
```

For faster searches of large directory trees, use find with xargs instead of grep -r:

```
$ vim $(find . -type f -print0 | xargs -0 grep -l string)
```

"Technique #3: Command Substitution" on page 110 touched on this technique, but I wanted to emphasize it since it's so useful. Remember to watch out for filenames containing spaces and other characters special to the shell, since they may disrupt the results as explained in "Special Characters and Command Substitution" on page 111.

Embracing Typos

If you consistently misspell a command, define aliases for your most common mistakes so the correct command runs anyway:

```
alias firfox=firefox
alias les=less
alias meacs=emacs
```

Be careful not to shadow (override) an existing Linux command accidentally by defining an alias with the same name. Search for your proposed alias first with the command which or type (see "Locating Programs to Be Run" on page 31), and run the man command to be extra sure there's no other same-named command:

```
$ type firfox
bash: type: firfox: not found
$ man firfox
No manual entry for firfox
```

Creating Empty Files Quickly

There are several ways to create empty files in Linux. The touch command, which updates the timestamp on a file, also creates a file if one doesn't already exist:

```
$ touch newfile1
```

touch is great for creating large numbers of empty files for testing:

```
$ mkdir tmp                          Create a directory
$ cd tmp
$ touch file{0000..9999}.txt         Create 10,000 files
$ cd ..
$ rm -rf tmp                         Remove the directory and files
```

The echo command creates an empty file if you redirect its output to a file, but only if you supply the -n option:

```
$ echo -n > newfile2
```

If you forget the -n option, the resulting file contains one character, a newline, so it's not empty.

Processing a File One Line at a Time

When you need to process a file one line at a time, cat the file into a while read loop:

```
$ cat myfile | while read line; do
  ...do something here...
done
```

For example, to compute the length of each line of a file, such as /etc/hosts, pipe each line to wc -c:

```
$ cat /etc/hosts | while read line; do
  echo "$line" | wc -c
done
65
31
1
⋮
```

A more practical example of this technique is in Example 9-3.

Identifying Commands That Support Recursion

In "The find Command" on page 71, I introduced find -exec, which applies any Linux command to a whole directory tree recursively:

```
$ find . -exec your command here \;
```

Certain other commands support recursion themselves, and if you're aware of them, you can save typing time by using their native recursion instead of constructing a find command:

```
ls -R
```
To list directories and their contents recursively

```
cp -r or cp -a
```
To copy directories and their contents recursively

```
rm -r
```
To delete directories and their contents recursively

```
grep -r
```
To search by regular expression throughout a directory tree

```
chmod -R
```
To change file protections recursively

```
chown -R
```
To change file ownership recursively

```
chgrp -R
```
To change file group ownership recursively

Read a Manpage

Pick a common command, such as cut or grep, and read its manpage thoroughly. You'll probably discover an option or two that you've never used and will find valuable. Repeat this activity every so often to polish and extend your Linux toolbox.

Longer Learning

The following techniques require real effort to learn, but you'll be paid back in time saved. I provide just a taste of each topic, not to teach you the details but to entice you to discover more on your own.

Read the bash Manpage

Run man bash to display the full, official documentation on bash, and read the whole thing—yes, all 46,318 words of it:

```
$ man bash | wc -w
46318
```

Take a few days. Work through it slowly. You'll definitely learn a lot to make your daily Linux use easier.

Learn cron, crontab, and at

In "A First Example: Finding Files" on page 155, there's a brief note about scheduling commands to run automatically in the future at regular intervals. I recommend learning the program `crontab` to set up scheduled commands for yourself. For example, you could back up files to an external drive on a schedule, or send yourself reminders by email for a monthly event.

Before running `crontab`, define your default editor as shown in "Jumping Into Your Editor from less" on page 189. Then run `crontab -e` to edit your personal file of scheduled commands. `crontab` launches your default editor and opens an empty file to specify the commands. That file is called your *crontab*.

Briefly, a scheduled command in a crontab file, often called a *cron job*, consists of six fields, all on a single (possibly long) line. The first five fields determine the job's schedule by minute, hour, day of month, month, and day of week, respectively. The sixth field is the Linux command to run. You can launch a command hourly, daily, weekly, monthly, yearly, at certain days or times, or in other more complex arrangements. Some examples are:

```
* * * * * command       Run command every minute
30 7 * * * command      Run command at 07:30 every day
30 7 5 * * command      Run command at 07:30 the 5th day of every month
30 7 5 1 * command      Run command at 07:30 every January 5
30 7 * * 1 command      Run command at 07:30 every Monday
```

Once you've created all six fields, saved the file, and exited your editor, the command is launched automatically (by a program called `cron`) according to the schedule you defined. The syntax for schedules is short and cryptic but well-documented on the manpage (`man 5 crontab`) and numerous online tutorials (search for *cron tutorial*).

I also recommend learning the `at` command, which schedules commands to run once, rather than repeatedly, at a specified date and time. Run `man at` for details. Here's a command that sends you an email reminder tomorrow at 10 p.m. to brush your teeth:

```
$ at 22:00 tomorrow
warning: commands will be executed using /bin/sh
at> echo brush your teeth | mail $USER
at> ^D                                  Type Ctrl-D to end input
job 699 at Sun Nov 14 22:00:00 2021
```

To list your pending `at` jobs, run `atq`:

```
$ atq
699     Sun Nov 14 22:00:00 2021 a smith
```

To view the commands in an `at` job, run `at -c` with the job number, and print the final few lines:

```
$ at -c 699 | tail
⋮
echo brush your teeth | mail $USER
```

To remove a pending job before it's executed, run `atrm` with the job number:

```
$ atrm 699
```

Learn rsync

To copy a full directory, including its subdirectories, from one disk location to another, many Linux users turn to the command `cp -r` or `cp -a`:

```
$ cp -a dir1 dir2
```

`cp` does the job fine the first time, but if you later modify a few files in directory *dir1* and perform the copy again, `cp` is wasteful. It dutifully copies all files and directories from *dir1* all over again, even if identical copies already exist in *dir2*.

The command `rsync` is a smarter copy program. It copies only the *differences* between the first and second directories.

```
$ rsync -a dir1/ dir2
```

 The forward slash in the preceding command means to copy the files inside *dir1*. Without the slash, `rsync` would copy *dir1* itself, creating *dir2/dir1*.

If you later add a file to directory *dir1*, `rsync` copies just that one file. If you change one *line* inside a file in *dir1*, `rsync` copies that one line! It's a huge time-saver when copying large directory trees multiple times. `rsync` can even copy to a remote server over an SSH connection.

`rsync` has dozens of options. These are some particularly useful ones:

-v *(meaning "verbose")*
   To print the names of files as they're copied

-n
   To pretend to copy; combine with -v to see which files *would* be copied

-x
   To tell `rsync` not to cross filesystem boundaries

I highly recommend getting comfortable with `rsync` for more efficient copying. Read the manpage and view examples in the article "Rsync Examples in Linux" (*https://oreil.ly/7gHCi*) by Korbin Brown.

Learn Another Scripting Language

Shell scripts are convenient and powerful but have some serious shortcomings. For example, they're terrible at handling filenames that contain whitespace characters. Consider this short `bash` script that attempts to remove a file:

```
#!/bin/bash
BOOKTITLE="Slow Inefficient Linux"
rm $BOOKTITLE                                # Wrong! Don't do this!
```

It looks like the second line removes a file named *Slow Inefficient Linux*, but it doesn't. It attempts to remove three files named *Slow*, *Inefficient*, and *Linux*. The shell expands the variable `$BOOKTITLE` before calling `rm`, and its expansion is three words separated by whitespace, as if you had typed the following:

```
rm Slow Inefficient Linux
```

The shell then invokes `rm` with three arguments, and potential disaster ensues as it removes the wrong files. A correct removal command would surround `$BOOKTITLE` with double quotes:

```
rm "$BOOKTITLE"
```

which the shell expands to:

```
rm "Slow Inefficient Linux"
```

This sort of subtle, potentially destructive quirk is just one example of how unsuitable shell scripting is for serious projects. So, I recommend learning a second scripting language, such as Perl, PHP, Python, or Ruby. They all handle whitespace properly. They all support real data structures. They all have powerful string-handling functions. They all do math easily. The list of benefits goes on.

Use the shell to launch complex commands and create simple scripts, but for more substantial tasks, turn to another language. Try one of the many language tutorials online.

Use make for Nonprogramming Tasks

The program `make` automatically updates files based on rules. It's designed to speed up software development, but with a little effort, `make` can simplify other aspects of your Linux life.

Suppose you have three files named *chapter1.txt*, *chapter2.txt*, and *chapter3.txt* that you work on separately. You also have a fourth file, *book.txt*, that's a combination of the three chapter files. Anytime a chapter changes, you need to recombine them and update *book.txt*, perhaps with a command like this:

```
$ cat chapter1.txt chapter2.txt chapter3.txt > book.txt
```

This situation is perfect for using make. You have:

- A bunch of files
- A rule that relates the files, namely, that *book.txt* needs an update whenever any chapter file changes
- A command that performs the update

make operates by reading a configuration file, usually named *Makefile*, that is full of rules and commands. For example, the following *Makefile* rule states that *book.txt* depends on the three chapter files:

```
book.txt:       chapter1.txt chapter2.txt chapter3.txt
```

If the target of the rule (in this case *book.txt*) is older than any of its dependencies (the chapter files), then make considers the target to be out-of-date. If you supply a command on the line after the rule, make runs the command to update the target:

```
book.txt:       chapter1.txt chapter2.txt chapter3.txt
                cat chapter1.txt chapter2.txt chapter3.txt > book.txt
```

To apply the rule, simply run the command make:

```
$ ls
Makefile  chapter1.txt  chapter2.txt  chapter3.txt
$ make
cat chapter1.txt chapter2.txt chapter3.txt > book.txt        Executed by make
$ ls
Makefile  book.txt  chapter1.txt  chapter2.txt  chapter3.txt
$ make
make: 'book.txt' is up to date.
$ vim chapter2.txt                                           Update a chapter
$ make
cat chapter1.txt chapter2.txt chapter3.txt > book.txt
```

make was developed for programmers, but with a little study, you can use it for non-programming tasks. Anytime you need to update files that depend on other files, you can likely simplify your work by writing a *Makefile*.

make helped me write and debug this book. I wrote the book in a typesetting language called AsciiDoc and regularly converted chapters to HTML to view in a browser. Here's a make rule to convert any AsciiDoc file to an HTML file:

```
%.html: %.asciidoc
        asciidoctor -o $@ $<
```

It means: to create a file with the extension *.html* (%.html), look for a corresponding file with the extension *.asciidoc* (%.asciidoc). If the HTML file is older than the AsciiDoc file, regenerate the HTML file by running the command asciidoctor on the dependent file ($<), sending the output to the target HTML file (-o $@). With this slightly cryptic but short rule in place, I type a simple `make` command to create the HTML version of the chapter you're reading now. `make` launches `asciidoctor` to perform the update:

```
$ ls ch11*
ch11.asciidoc
$ make ch11.html
asciidoctor -o ch11.html ch11.asciidoc
$ ls ch11*
ch11.asciidoc  ch11.html
$ firefox ch11.html                          View the HTML file
```

It takes less than an hour to become reasonably proficient with `make` for small tasks. It's worth the effort. A helpful guide is at makefiletutorial.com.

Apply Version Control to Day-to-Day Files

Have you ever wanted to edit a file but were afraid that your changes might mess it up? Perhaps you made a backup copy for safekeeping and edited the original, knowing you could restore the backup if you make a mistake:

```
$ cp myfile myfile.bak
```

This solution isn't scalable. What if you have dozens or hundreds of files and dozens or hundreds of people working on them? Version control systems such as Git and Subversion were invented to solve this problem in general by tracking multiple versions of a file conveniently.

Git is widespread for maintaining software source code, but I recommend learning and using it for any important text files where your changes matter. Perhaps they're personal files, or operating system files in */etc*. "Traveling with Your Environment" on page 106 suggests maintaining your `bash` configuration files with version control.

I used Git while writing this book so I could try different ways of presenting the material. Without too much effort, I created and maintained three different versions of the book—one for the full manuscript so far, one containing only the chapters I'd submitted to my editor for review, and one for experimental work where I tried out new ideas. If I didn't like what I wrote, a single command would restore a previous version.

Teaching Git is beyond the scope of this book, but here are some example commands to show you the basic workflow and whet your appetite. Convert the current directory (and all its subdirectories) into a Git repository:

```
$ git init
```

Edit some files. Afterward, add the changed files to an invisible "staging area," an operation that declares your intent to create a new version:

```
$ git add .
```

Create the new version, providing a comment to describe your changes to the files:

```
$ git commit -m"Changed X to Y"
```

View your version history:

```
$ git log
```

There's much more to it, like retrieving old versions of files and saving (*pushing*) versions to another server. Grab a `git` tutorial (*https://oreil.ly/0AlOu*), and get started!

Farewell

Thank you so much for following along with me through this book. I hope it has fulfilled the promise I made in the preface to take your Linux command-line skills to the next level. Tell me about your experience at *dbarrett@oreilly.com*. Happy computing.

Linux Refresher

If your Linux skills are rusty, here's a very quick review of some details you'll need for this book. (If you're a complete beginner, this review might be too brief. Check out the recommended reading at the end.)

Commands, Arguments, and Options

To run a Linux command at the command line, type the command and press Enter. To kill a command in progress, press Ctrl-C.

A simple Linux command consists of a single word, which is usually the name of a program, followed by additional strings called *arguments*. For example, the following command consists of a program name, ls, and two arguments:

```
$ ls -l /bin
```

Arguments that begin with a dash, such as -l, are called *options* because they change the command's behavior. Other arguments might be filenames, directory names, usernames, hostnames, or any other strings that the program needs. Options usually (but not always) precede the rest of the arguments.

Command options come in various forms, depending on which program you run:

- A single letter, such as -l, sometimes followed by a value, as in -n 10. Usually the space between the letter and the value can be omitted: -n10.

- A word preceded by two dashes, such as --long, sometimes followed by a value, as in --block-size 100. The space between the option and its value may often be replaced by an equals sign: --block-size=100.

- A word preceded by one dash, such as -type, optionally followed by a value, as in -type f. This option format is rare; one command that uses it is find.

- A single letter without a dash. This option format is rare; one command that uses it is tar.

Multiple options may often (depending on the command) be combined behind a single dash. For example, the command ls -al is equivalent to ls -a -l.

Options vary not only in appearance but also in meaning. In the command ls -l, the -l means "long output," but in the command wc -l it means "lines of text." Two programs also might use different options to mean the same thing, such as -q for "run quietly" versus -s for "run silently." Inconsistencies like these make Linux harder to learn, but you eventually get used to them.

The Filesystem, Directories, and Paths

Linux files are contained in directories (folders) that are organized into a tree structure, such as the one in Figure A-1. The tree begins in a directory called the *root*, denoted by a single forward slash (/), which may contain files and other directories, called *subdirectories*. For example, the directory *Music* has two subdirectories, *mp3* and *SheetMusic*. We call *Music* the parent directory of *mp3* and *SheetMusic*. Directories with the same parent are called *siblings*.

A path through the tree is written as a sequence of directory names separated by forward slashes, such as */home/smith/Music/mp3*. A path may also end with a filename, as in */home/smith/Music/mp3/catalog.txt*. These paths are called *absolute paths* because they begin at the root directory. Paths that begin elsewhere (and don't start with a forward slash) are called *relative paths* because they are relative to the current directory. If your current directory is */home/smith/Music*, then some relative paths are *mp3* (a subdirectory) and *mp3/catalog.txt* (a file). Even a filename by itself, like *catalog.txt*, is a relative path with respect to */home/smith/Music/mp3*.

Two special relative paths are a single dot (.), which refers to the current directory, and two dots in a row (..), which refers to the current directory's parent.[1] Both can be part of larger paths. For example, if your current directory is */home/smith/Music/mp3*, then the path .. refers to *Music*, the path ../../../.. refers to the root directory, and the path ../SheetMusic refers to a sibling of *mp3*.

---

[1] The dot and double dot are not expressions evaluated by the shell. They are hard links present in every directory.

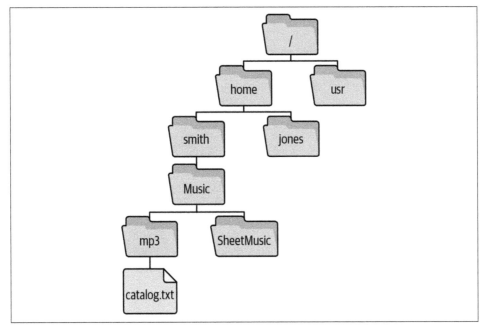

Figure A-1. Paths in a Linux directory tree

You and every other user on a Linux system have a designated directory, called your *home directory*, where you can freely create, edit, and delete files and directories. Its path is usually */home/* followed by your username, such as */home/smith*.

Directory Movement

At any moment, your command line (shell) operates in a given directory, called your *current directory*, *working directory*, or *current working directory*. View the path of your current directory with the pwd (print working directory) command:

```
$ pwd
/home/smith                    The home directory of user smith
```

Move between directories with the cd (change directory) command, supplying the path (absolute or relative) to your desired destination:

```
$ cd /usr/local      Absolute path
$ cd bin             Relative path leading to /usr/local/bin
$ cd ../etc          Relative path leading to /usr/local/etc
```

Creating and Editing Files

Edit files with a standard Linux text editor by running any of the following commands:

`emacs`
> Once emacs is running, type Ctrl-h followed by t for a tutorial.

`nano`
> Visit nano-editor.org for documentation.

`vim` *or* `vi`
> Run the command `vimtutor` for a tutorial.

To create a file, simply provide its name as an argument, and the editor creates it:

```
$ nano newfile.txt
```

Alternatively, create an empty file with the `touch` command, supplying the desired filename as an argument:

```
$ touch funky.txt
$ ls
funky.txt
```

File and Directory Handling

List the files in a directory (by default, your current directory) with the `ls` command:

```
$ ls
animals.txt
```

See attributes of a file or directory with a "long" listing (`ls -l`):

```
$ ls -l
-rw-r--r-- 1 smith smith  325 Jul  3 17:44 animals.txt
```

Left to right, the attributes are the file permissions (`-rw-r—r--`) described in "File Permissions" on page 204, the owner (`smith`) and group (`smith`), the size in bytes (`325`), the last modification date and time (`Jul  3` of this year at `17:44`), and the filename (`animals.txt`).

By default, `ls` does not print filenames that begin with a dot. To list these files, which are often called *dot files* or *hidden files*, add the `-a` option:

```
$ ls -a
.bashrc     .bash_profile    animals.txt
```

Copy a file with the `cp` command, supplying the original filename and the new filename:

```
$ cp animals.txt beasts.txt
$ ls
animals.txt    beasts.txt
```

Rename a file with the `mv` (move) command, supplying the original filename and the new filename:

```
$ mv beasts.txt creatures.txt
$ ls
animals.txt    creatures.txt
```

Delete a file with the `rm` (remove) command:

```
$ rm creatures.txt
```

 Deletion on Linux is not friendly. The `rm` command does not ask "Are you sure?" and there is no trash can for restoring files.

Create a directory with `mkdir`, rename it with `mv`, and delete it (if empty) with `rmdir`:

```
$ mkdir testdir
$ ls
animals.txt    testdir
$ mv testdir newname
$ ls
animals.txt    newname
$ rmdir newname
$ ls
animals.txt
```

Copy one or more files (or directories) into a directory:

```
$ touch file1 file2 file3
$ mkdir dir
$ ls
dir    file1    file2    file3
$ cp file1 file2 file3 dir
$ ls
dir    file1    file2    file3
$ ls dir
file1    file2    file3
$ rm file1 file2 file3
```

Continuing, move one or more files (or directories) into a directory:

```
$ touch thing1 thing2 thing3
$ ls
dir    thing1    thing2    thing3
$ mv thing1 thing2 thing3 dir
$ ls
dir
$ ls dir
file1    file2    file3    thing1    thing2    thing3
```

Delete a directory and all its contents with rm -rf. Take care before running this command because it is not reversible. See "Never Delete the Wrong File Again (Thanks to History Expansion)" on page 41 for safety tips.

```
$ rm -rf dir
```

File Viewing

Print a text file on the screen with the cat command:

```
$ cat animals.txt
```

View a text file one screenful at a time with the less command:

```
$ less animals.txt
```

While running less, display the next page by pressing the spacebar. To exit less, press q. For help, press h.

File Permissions

The chmod command sets a file to be readable, writable, and/or executable by yourself, a given group of users, or everybody. Figure A-2 is a brief refresher on file permissions.

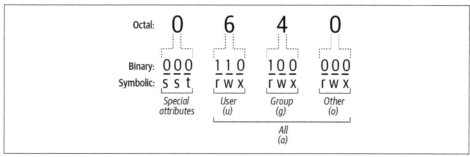

Figure A-2. File permission bits

Here are some common operations with chmod. Make a file readable and writable by you, and only readable by everyone else:

```
$ chmod 644 animals.txt
$ ls -l
-rw-r--r-- 1 smith smith  325 Jul  3 17:44 animals.txt
```

Protect it from all other users:

```
$ chmod 600 animals.txt
$ ls -l
-rw------- 1 smith smith  325 Jul  3 17:44 animals.txt
```

Make a directory readable and enterable by everyone, but writable only by you:

```
$ mkdir dir
$ chmod 755 dir
$ ls -l
drwxr-xr-x 2 smith smith  4096 Oct  1 12:44 dir
```

Protect a directory from all other users:

```
$ chmod 700 dir
$ ls -l
drwx------ 2 smith smith  4096 Oct  1 12:44 dir
```

Normal permissions don't apply to the superuser, who can read and write all files and directories on the system.

Processes

When you run a Linux command, it launches one or more Linux *processes*, each with a numeric process ID called a *PID*. See your shell's current processes with the ps command:

```
$ ps
    PID TTY          TIME CMD
   5152 pts/11   00:00:00 bash
 117280 pts/11   00:00:00 emacs
 117273 pts/11   00:00:00 ps
```

or all running processes for all users with:

```
$ ps -uax
```

Kill a process of your own with the kill command, supplying the PID as an argument. The superuser (Linux administrator) can kill any user's process.

```
$ kill 117280
[1]+  Exit 15                 emacs animals.txt
```

Viewing Documentation

The `man` command prints documentation about any standard command on your Linux system. Simply type `man` followed by the name of the command. For example, to view documentation for the `cat` command, run the following:

```
$ man cat
```

The displayed document is known as the command's *manpage*. When someone says "view the manpage for grep," they mean run the command `man grep`.

`man` displays documentation one page at a time using the program `less`,[2] so the standard keystrokes for `less` will work. Table A-1 lists some common keystrokes.

Table A-1. Some keystrokes for viewing manpages with `less`

Keystroke	Action
h	Help—display a list of keystrokes for `less`
spacebar	View the next page
b	View the previous page
Enter	Scroll down one line
<	Jump to the beginning of the document
>	Jump to the end of the document
/	Search forward for text (type the text and press Enter)
?	Search backward for text (type the text and press Enter)
n	Locate the next occurrence of the search text
q	Quit `man`

Shell Scripts

To run a bunch of Linux commands as a unit, follow these steps:

1. Place the commands in a file.
2. Insert a magical first line.
3. Make the file executable with `chmod`.
4. Execute the file.

---

2 Or another program if you redefine the value of the shell variable PAGER.

The file is called a *script* or *shell script*. The magical first line should be the symbols #! (pronounced "shebang") followed by the path to a program that reads and runs the script:[3]

```
#!/bin/bash
```

Here is a shell script that says hello and prints today's date. Lines beginning with # are comments:

```
#!/bin/bash
# This is a sample script
echo "Hello there!"
date
```

Use a text editor to store these lines in a file called *howdy*. Then make the file executable by running either of these commands:

```
$ chmod 755 howdy      Set all permissions, including execute permission
$ chmod +x howdy       Or, just add execute permission
```

and run it:

```
$ ./howdy
Hello there!
Fri Sep 10 17:00:52 EDT 2021
```

The leading dot and slash (./) indicate that the script is in your current directory. Without them, the Linux shell won't find the script:[4]

```
$ howdy
howdy: command not found
```

Linux shells provide some programming language features that are useful in scripts. bash, for example, provides if statements, for loops, while loops, and other control structures. A few examples are sprinkled throughout the book. See man bash for the syntax.

Becoming the Superuser

Some files, directories, and programs are protected from normal users, including you:

```
$ touch /usr/local/avocado       Try to create a file in a system directory
touch: cannot touch '/usr/local/avocado': Permission denied
```

---

3 If you omit the shebang line, your default shell will run the script. It's a good practice to include the line.

4 That's because the current directory is usually omitted from the shell's search path, for security reasons. Otherwise, an attacker could place a malicious, executable script named ls in your current directory, and when you ran ls, the script would run instead of the true ls command.

"Permission denied" usually means you tried to access protected resources. They are accessible only to the Linux superuser (username root). Most Linux systems come with a program called sudo (pronounced "soo doo") that lets you become the superuser for the duration of a single command. If you installed Linux yourself, your account is probably set up already to run sudo. If you're one user on somebody else's Linux system, you might not have superuser privileges; speak to your system administrator if you're not sure.

Assuming you're set up properly, simply run sudo, supplying it with the desired command to run as the superuser. You'll be prompted for your login password to prove your identity. Supply it correctly, and the command will run with root privileges:

```
$ sudo touch /usr/local/avocado              Create the file as root
[sudo] password for smith: password here
$ ls -l /usr/local/avocado                   List the file
-rw-r--r-- 1 root root 0 Sep 10 17:16 avocado
$ sudo rm /usr/local/avocado                 Clean up as root
```

sudo may remember (cache) your passphrase for a while, depending on how sudo is configured, so it might not prompt you every time.

Further Reading

For more basics of Linux use, read my previous book, *Linux Pocket Guide* (O'Reilly), or seek out online tutorials (*https://oreil.ly/KLTji*).

If You Use a Different Shell

This book assumes your login shell is bash, but if it's not, Table B-1 may help you adapt the book's examples for other shells. The checkmark symbol ✓ indicates compatibility—the given feature is similar enough to bash's that examples in the book should run correctly. However, the feature's behavior may differ from bash's in other ways. Read any footnotes carefully.

Regardless of which shell is your login shell, scripts that begin with #!/bin/bash are processed by bash.

To experiment with another shell installed on your system, simply run it by name (e.g., ksh) and press Ctrl-D when finished. To change your login shell, read man chsh.

Table B-1. bash features supported by other shells, in alphabetical order

bash feature	dash	fish	ksh	tcsh	zsh
alias builtin	✓	✓, but alias *name* does not print the alias	✓	No equals sign: alias g grep	✓
Backgrounding with &	✓	✓	✓	✓	✓
bash -c	dash -c	fish -c	ksh -c	tcsh -c	zsh -c
bash command	dash	fish	ksh	tcsh	zsh
bash location in */bin/ bash*	*/bin/dash*	*/bin/fish*	*/bin/ksh*	*/bin/tcsh*	*/bin/zsh*

bash feature	dash	fish	ksh	tcsh	zsh
BASH_SUBSHELL variable					
Brace expansion with {}	Use seq	Only {a,b,c}, not {a..c}	✓	Use seq	✓
cd - (toggling directories)	✓	✓	✓	✓	✓
cd builtin	✓	✓	✓	✓	✓
CDPATH variable	✓	set CDPATH value	✓	set cdpath = (dir1 dir2 …)	✓
Command substitution with $()	✓	Use ()	✓	Use backquotes	✓
Command substitution with backquotes	✓	Use ()	✓	✓	✓
Command-line editing with arrow keys		✓	✓[a]	✓	✓
Command-line editing with Emacs keys		✓	✓[a]	✓	✓
Command-line editing with Vim keys with set -o vi			✓	Run bindkey -v	✓
complete builtin		different syntax[b]	different syntax[b]	different syntax[b]	compdef[b]
Conditional lists with && and ||	✓	✓	✓	✓	✓
Configuration files in $HOME (read manpage for details)	.profile	.config/fish/config.fish	.profile, .kshrc	.tcshrc, .cshrc, .login	.zshenv, .zprofile, .zshrc, .zlogin, .zlogout
Control structures: for loops, if statements, etc.	✓	different syntax	✓	different syntax	✓
dirs builtin		✓		✓	✓
echo builtin	✓	✓	✓	✓	✓
Escape alias with \	✓		✓	✓	✓
Escape with \	✓	✓	✓	✓	✓
exec builtin	✓	✓	✓	✓	✓
Exit code with $?	✓	$status	✓	✓	✓
export builtin	✓	set -x name value	✓	setenv name value	✓
Functions	✓[c]	different syntax	✓		✓

bash feature	dash	fish	ksh	tcsh	zsh
HISTCONTROL variable					See variables with names beginning in HIST_ on the manpage
HISTFILE variable		set fish_history *path*	✓	set histfile = *path*	✓
HISTFILESIZE variable				set savehist = *value*	+SAVEHIST
history builtin		✓, but commands are not numbered	history is an alias for hist -l	✓	✓
history -c		history clear	Delete *~/.sh_history* and restart ksh	✓	history -p
History expansion with ! and ^				✓	✓
History incremental search with Ctrl-R		Type beginning of command, then press up arrow to search, right arrow to select	✓[a][d]	✓[e]	✓[f]
history *number*		history -*number*	history -N *number*	✓	history -*number*
History with arrow keys		✓	✓[a]	✓	✓
History with Emacs keys		✓	✓[a]	✓	✓
History with Vim keys with set -o vi			✓	Run bindkey -v	✓
HISTSIZE variable			✓		✓
Job control with fg, bg, Ctrl-Z, jobs	✓	✓	✓	✓[g]	✓
Pattern matching with *, ?, []	✓	✓	✓	✓	✓
Pipes	✓	✓	✓	✓	✓
popd builtin		✓		✓	✓
Process substitution with <()			✓		✓
PS1 variable	✓	set PS1 *value*	✓	set prompt = *value*	✓
pushd builtin		✓		✓, but no negative arguments	✓
Quotes, double	✓	✓	✓	✓	✓

bash feature	dash	fish	ksh	tcsh	zsh
Quotes, single	✓	✓	✓	✓	✓
Redirection of stderr (2>)	✓	✓	✓		✓
Redirection of stdin (<), stdout (>, >>)	✓	✓	✓	✓	✓
Redirection of stdout + stderr (&>)	Append 2>&1[h]	✓	Append 2>&1[h]	>&	✓
Sourcing a file with source or . (dot)	dot only[i]	✓	✓[i]	source only	✓[i]
Subshell with ( )	✓		✓	✓	✓
Tab completion for filenames		✓	✓[a]	✓	✓
type builtin	✓	✓	type is an alias for whence -v	No, but which is a builtin	✓
unalias builtin	✓	functions --erase	✓	✓	✓
Variable definition with name=value	✓	set *name value*	✓	set *name = value*	✓
Variable evaluation with $name	✓	✓	✓	✓	✓

[a] This feature is disabled by default. Run set -o emacs to enable it. Older versions of ksh may behave differently.

[b] Custom command completion, using the complete command or similar, differs significantly from shell to shell; read the shell's manpage.

[c] Functions: This shell does not support newer-style definitions that begin with the function keyword.

[d] Incremental search of history works differently in ksh. Press Ctrl-R, type a string, and press Enter to recall the most recent command containing that string. Press Ctrl-R and Enter again to search backward for the next matching command, and so on. Press Enter to execute.

[e] To enable incremental history search with Ctrl-R in tcsh, run the command bindkey ^R i-search-back (and add it to a shell configuration file). The search behavior is a bit different from bash's; see man tcsh.

[f] In vi mode, type / followed by the search string, then press Enter. Press n to jump to the next search result.

[g] Job control: tcsh does not track the default job number as intelligently as other shells, so you may need to supply the job number, such as %1, as an argument to fg and bg more often.

[h] Redirection of stdout and stderr: The syntax in this shell is: *command* > *file* 2>&1. The final term 2>&1 means "redirect stderr, which is file descriptor 2, to stdout, which is file descriptor 1."

[i] Sourcing in this shell requires an explicit path to the sourced file, such as ./myfile for a file in the current directory, or the shell won't locate the file. Alternatively, place the file into a directory in the shell's search path.

Index

(see also conditional lists)
vi (see vim editor)
viewing files, 204
   one screenful at a time, 4, 204
vim editor, 202
   exiting, 189
   tutorial, 202
   vim-gnupg plugin, 166
vimtutor command, 202
virtual desktops, 174
visiting a directory, 50
VISUAL variable, 189

W

wc command, 6
   character counting (-c option), 6
   examples, 68, 139, 147, 148, 159, 185
   line counting (-l option), 6
   reading from stdin, 7
   word counting (-w option), 6
web browser
   downloading pages with text-based, 182
   downloading pages without, 177
   keyboard shortcuts, 173
     new window, 171
   launching from command line, 175
     arguments, 175
     incognito/private, 175
   text-based, 182
   user agent, 177
web pages
   downloading, 177-183
   parsing HTML, 178
   suspicious-looking links, 183
wget command, 177
which command, 32
while loop, 207
   while read, 157, 176, 191
whitespace
   awk handling of, 79
   deleting, 71, 84
   filenames containing, 111
   scripting languages handling, 195
   separator, 29, 122
   significant, 29
   variables defined without, 24
whois command, 156
Wikipedia software, 143
wildcards, 19

(see also pattern matching)
windows
   opening with keyboard shortcut, 172
   switching, 174
words file (see dictionary file)
working directory (see current directory)
wrapping text, 93

X

X (windowing software), 183
   configuration file, 105
X selections
   appending, 186
   clearing, 185, 186
   from command line, 183
xargs command, 120
   examples, 150, 154, 178
   filename pattern matching versus, 121
   find command with, 121, 190
   input string separators, 122
   maximum arguments per command line (-n
     option), 121
   null separators (-0 option), 121
   piping commands to bash versus, 178
   replacement string (-I option), 123
   safety, 122
   solving "argument list too long" error, 123
xclip command, 184
   abbreviating options, 185
   choose selection (--selection option), 185
   output (-o option), 184
.xinitrc file, 105
xsel command, 186
xterm command, 172

Y

yes command, 73
   examples, 149
yum package manager, 94

Z

zero
   ASCII zero as null character, 122
   leading, 69, 70
   string length test, 163
zsh shell, xi, 209
zypper package manager, 94

About the Author

Daniel J. Barrett has been teaching and writing about Linux and related technologies for more than 30 years. He is an author of numerous O'Reilly books such as *Linux Pocket Guide, Linux Security Cookbook, SSH, The Secure Shell: The Definitive Guide, Macintosh Terminal Pocket Guide*, and *MediaWiki*. Dan has also been a software engineer, heavy metal singer, system administrator, university lecturer, web designer, and humorist. He works at Google. Visit DanielJBarrett.com to learn more.

Colophon

The animal on the cover of *Efficient Linux at the Command Line* is a saker falcon (*Falco cherrug*).

Swift, powerful, and aggressive, these large raptors have been prized by falconers for thousands of years. Today, they are the celebrated national bird of several countries, including Hungary, Mongolia, and the United Arab Emirates.

Adult sakers often reach 45–57 cm (18–22 in) in size, with broad wings spanning 97–126 cm (38–50 in). Females of the species are significantly larger than males, weighing 970–1,300 g (34–46 oz) as compared to 730–990 g (26–35 oz) for the latter. The plumage of both sexes is highly variable, ranging from deep brown to pale tan, or even white, with brown streaks or bars.

In the wild, sakers hunt primarily birds and rodents, achieving flight speeds of up to 120–150 km/h (75–93 mph) before swooping on their prey. Typical habitats include grasslands, cliffsides, and gallery forests, where the falcons occupy nests abandoned by other birds. With some exceptions in their ranges' southernmost areas, sakers are migratory birds, traveling annually from eastern Europe and central Asia to northern parts of Africa and southern Asia for the winter.

Other than humans, sakers have no known predators in the wild. Yet, due to rapid population decline, the saker falcon is now classified as endangered, as are many of the animals on O'Reilly covers. All of them are important to the world.

The cover illustration is by Karen Montgomery, based on an antique line engraving from Lydekker's *The Royal Natural History*. The cover fonts are Gilroy Semibold and Guardian Sans. The text font is Adobe Minion Pro; the heading font is Adobe Myriad Condensed; and the code font is Dalton Maag's Ubuntu Mono.

Milton Keynes UK
Ingram Content Group UK Ltd.
UKHW051556210924
448609UK00003B/15